Condiments!

Condiments!
Chutneys, Relishes, and Table Sauces

by Jay Solomon

Specialty Cookbook Series Edited by Andrea Chesman

The Crossing Press • Freedom, California 95019

*This book is dedicated to my grandmother, Mary Badia Solomon,
and to my best friend, Dr. Janet Welch.*

Copyright © 1990 by Jay Solomon
Cover illustration and design by Betsy Bayley
Text illustrations by Melanie Lofland Gendron

Library of Congress Cataloging-in-Publication Data

Solomon, Jay
    Condiments! : chutneys, relishes, and table sauces / by Jay Solomon
      p. cm. -- (Specialty cookbook series)
    Includes index.
    ISBN 0-89594-444-8 -- ISBN 0-89594-443-X
    1. Condiments. I. Title. II. Series.
  TX819.A1S65 1990
  641.6'382--dc20
                                      90-2398
                                      CIP

Contents

Preface

✛✛

This cookbook grew out of my passion for condiments. I fill my day preparing salsa, Creole sauce, and garlicky aioli. I make chutney on a daily basis the way other chefs make soup. I make condiments for every occasion, from soothing raitas, sweet and tart relishes, robust catsups, fiery red chili sauces, and piquant mustards.

I use condiments in a variety of ways. They add flair to soups in the winter, salads in the spring, barbecues in the summer, and roasts in the fall. Condiments add zest to a wide array of chicken, fish, seafood, pork, and beef entrées. Condiments also inspire and embellish vegetarian meals.

Most are easy to prepare and don't require esoteric ingredients or time-consuming cooking techniques. In addition, condiments can be made ahead of time so that complexly flavored dishes can be quickly and easily assembled at mealtime. Once you discover fruity chutneys and catsups, feisty salsas, bold relishes, flavored mayonnaises and mustards, and exotic international sauces, you'll say good-bye to gooey gravy and fragile hollandaise. The condiments in this book throw the door open to healthy and innovative meals perfect for our times.

I view cooking as an art form in which anyone can participate and enjoy. The dinner plate is the canvas; fresh, healthy ingredients are the colors; and the stove top or grill is the palette. Follow these recipes, mix the colors, improvise a little, and a produce a culinary masterpiece! That's what this cookbook is all about: cooking creatively with condiments, eating well, and having fun.

Like the newspaper reporter who dreams of writing the great American novel, or the local musician who dreams of a record contract, chefs aspire to a cookbook, to share his or her ideas and specialties with others. Here is my cookbook. It is the culmination of many hours of dicing, slicing, cooking, tasting, measuring, and critiquing recipes for condiments.

Acknowledgments

There are many people who have encouraged and supported me in my culinary endeavors. I would like to thank Andrea Chesman, my editor, for her sound judgment and guidance. I would also like to thank Elaine Gill for giving me the opportunity to write this book. My grandmother, father, mother, brother, sister, and many other relatives have always given me useful advice. Several friends and staff have helped me over the years: Robert Cima, Shaun "Guy" Buckley, Ruth Townsend, Frank Folino, Jessica and Emily Robin, Lauren Cramer, Michael Kraft, Lisa and Michele Van Hoeck, Annie Burns, Marion Cardwell, Robinne Gray, Marilee Gauger Murphy, James Paradiso, Peggy and Tammy Livengood, Adrienne Nims, and the many loyal customers of Jay's Café in Ithaca. Special thanks to Irene Zahava of Smedley's Bookshop and Linda McCandless of *The Grapevine Weekly*, who encouraged me to pursue this project. Genene Boldt of BOCES Adult Education and the students who have taken my cooking classes have helped me refine my style of cooking. Jeff Lischer and Helen Scammell have faithfully assisted me in the kitchen for the past year, and I am greatly indebted to them. And, of course, I owe a tremendous debt of gratitude to my best friend, Dr. Janet Welch. Her sense of humor, wit, and advice have been a welcome reprieve from the restaurant world and have enabled me to keep things in proper perspective.

1
Salsas

✢✢✢

Some people find bliss in chocolate. Others find it in a carrot pulled from the garden, or an apple plucked from a tree. I find joy in extremely spicy food. Chili peppers make my day.

Salsa, which means "sauce" in Spanish, is a traditional Mexican condiment. Many people think of salsa as a peppery tomato dip served with tortilla chips, but it is much, much more than that. Salsa can be made with a variety of fruit and vegetables, and it can accompany a wide range of dishes, from grilled fish, steak, and chicken, to flour tortillas stuffed with pesto and shrimp.

Although the salsas I create are not authentic Mexican salsas, they capture the spirit of salsa. Fresh chili peppers, fresh cilantro, and lime juice are the core ingredients. This trio of flavors leaves a well-rounded zing at the tip of the tongue. Tomatoes and tomatillos (Mexican green tomatoes) make the heartiest salsas, while fresh fruits, such as pineapple, kiwi, raspberry, and papaya, make tangy, light salsas.

Many of the recipes here can be tailored to your individual tastes. I like to add more jalapeño peppers to my salsa and spike it with a generous amount of red hot sauce. Others might prefer more cilantro or lime juice. The degree of heat is up to you.

The hearty salsas in this chapter—Red Tomato Salsa; Avocado, Black Bean, and Corn Salsa; and Tomatillo Salsa—make the best condiments for stuffed tortillas. Tortillas, unleavened, thin breads made from corn or wheat flour, are a staple of Mexican cuisine. Tortillas wrap a variety of ingredients—chicken, pork, seafood, cheese, and vegetables—similar to an egg roll or crêpe. Burritos, enchiladas, tacos, and quesadillas are all made with tortillas.

The fresh fruit salsas in this chapter, including Raspberry Salsa, Pineapple-Kiwi Salsa, and Papaya-Tomatillo Salsa, make light, tangy accompaniments to grilled chicken, fish, pork, and steamed vegetables. They are sprightly alternatives to rich, hackneyed sauces, such as hollandaise and tartar sauce.

Red Tomato Salsa

❖❖

2 tomatoes, diced
1 green pepper, seeded and diced
1 medium-size onion, diced
1 tablespoon minced fresh cilantro
2 to 3 garlic cloves, minced
1 to 2 jalapeño peppers, seeded and
  minced
2 teaspoons lime juice
1 teaspoon ground cumin
1 teaspoon dried oregano
1 teaspoon red hot sauce
¼ teaspoon black pepper
¼ teaspoon white pepper
¼ teaspoon salt
¼ teaspoon dried red pepper flakes
¼ teaspoon cayenne pepper
2 cups canned crushed tomatoes

Combine all of the ingredients, except the crushed tomatoes, in a large bowl and mix well. Place three-quarters of the mixture in a food processor fitted with a steel blade and process for 5 seconds, creating a vegetable mash.

Return the mash to the bowl, add the crushed tomatoes, and blend well.

Wrap the salsa tightly and chill for at least 1 hour to allow the flavors to blend. If refrigerated, this salsa will keep for about 7 days.

YIELD: 4 CUPS

Tomatillo Salsa

✚✚✚

Tomatillos, also known as green tomatoes, are tart like a young, green apple. They are native to Mexico and not related to tomatoes or apples. Because of their sour, almost lime-like taste, they are often juxtaposed with more biting flavors like hot chili peppers and cilantro. They make an ideal medium for an extra-spicy salsa, a salsa on the edge.

6 medium-size fresh tomatillos, diced (available where specialty food is sold)
3 medium-size tomatoes, diced
½ cup minced red onion
2 garlic cloves, minced
2 to 3 jalapeño peppers, seeded and minced

1 tablespoon minced fresh cilantro
½ teaspoon ground cumin
⅛ teaspoon salt
⅛ teaspoon cayenne pepper

Combine all of the ingredients and mix well. Chill for at least 1 hour before serving. If refrigerated, this salsa should keep for 5 to 7 days.

YIELD: 3½ CUPS

Papaya-Tomatillo Salsa

✦✦

Sweet papayas and tart tomatillos make a perfect yin-yang salsa. This refreshing salsa goes well with grilled fish and chicken.

1 medium-size papaya, peeled, seeded, and diced
4 to 5 tomatillos, diced
2 jalapeño peppers, seeded and minced
1 unwaxed cucumber, diced (do not peel)
½ cup minced red onion
¼ cup lime juice
2 tablespoons minced fresh cilantro
¼ teaspoon salt

Combine all of the ingredients and mix well. Chill for at least 1 hour before serving. If refrigerated, this salsa should keep for about 4 days.

Note: If you can't find unwaxed cucumbers, substitute waxed cucumbers but peel them first. You can also use about 1 cup of unpeeled, diced European cucumber.

YIELD: 3½ CUPS

Pineapple-Kiwi Salsa

❖❖

Kiwi is an exotic fruit that was once hard to find but is now readily available in most markets. Underneath its scruffy brown exterior lies a vibrant lime-green pulp that exudes a flavor which is a cross between a banana and a strawberry. Combined with pineapple, it makes a crisp, citrusy condiment which is great with mildly flavored fish, such as salmon or mahimahi.

½ medium-size pineapple, peeled, cored, and diced
4 kiwis, peeled and diced
1 fresh red chili pepper, seeded and minced
1 tablespoon minced fresh cilantro
1 tablespoon lemon juice or lime juice

Combine all of the ingredients in a bowl and mix well. Chill for at least 2 hours before serving. If refrigerated, this salsa should keep for 4 to 5 days.

YIELD: 3 CUPS

Raspberry Salsa

✦✦✦

Raspberry salsa makes a vivid accompaniment to grilled fish, grilled chicken, stuffed tortillas, and crêpes. I like to spoon it over steamed asparagus and carrots. The slightly tart raspberries form a delectable alliance with the cilantro, vinegar, and jalapeño peppers.

2 cups fresh or unsweetened frozen,
   thawed, and drained raspberries
2 jalapeño peppers, seeded and minced
2 tablespoons minced red onion
2 tablespoons minced fresh cilantro
2 tablespoons red wine vinegar
⅛ teaspoon salt

Combine all of the ingredients in a mixing bowl and chill for 1 hour. If refrigerated, this salsa should keep for about 7 days.

YIELD: 2 CUPS

Corn & Black Bean Salsa

✤✤✤

Spoon this hearty, colorful salsa over a baked potato or winter squash or add it to a tossed salad. Serve it with grilled trout, salmon, chicken, or, of course, a stuffed tortilla. Or simply fill a taco with shredded cheese, lettuce, and the salsa.

2 tomatoes, diced
1 ripe avocado, peeled and chopped
1 to 2 jalapeño peppers, seeded and
   minced
1 green pepper, seeded and diced
1 cup corn kernels, fresh, canned, or
   frozen and thawed
½ cup cooked black beans (page 169)
¼ cup diced red onion
1 tablespoon minced fresh cilantro

1 tablespoon lime juice
1 teaspoon ground cumin
½ teaspoon red hot sauce
⅛ teaspoon salt
⅛ teaspoon cayenne pepper

Combine all of the ingredients in a large bowl and blend well. Serve at once or wrap tightly and chill. If refrigerated, the salsa should keep for 3 to 4 days.

YIELD: 4 CUPS

Jicama Salad

❖❖❖

The wedding of salsa and vinaigrette results in a tasty, tangy salad dressing. Spoon it over fresh greens or marinate mixed vegetables with it. Jicama, also known as Mexican potato, is a favorite salad ingredient because it refuses to wilt and remains moist and crunchy for days.

3 tablespoons red wine vinegar
2 teaspoons Dijon-style mustard
½ cup vegetable or olive oil
½ cup Raspberry Salsa (page 7)
12 asparagus stalks
½ pound jicama, peeled and cut into
  ¼-inch matchsticks
2 (5-inch to 6-inch) carrots, cut
  lengthwise into matchsticks
4 leaves leaf or romaine lettuce

Whisk the vinegar and mustard together. Gradually whisk the oil into the mixture. Add the salsa and whisk until fully incorporated. Pour into a mixing bowl.

Blanch the asparagus in boiling water to cover for 2 minutes. Drain and chill under cold running water.

Combine the asparagus, jicama, and carrots with the vinaigrette and toss thoroughly. Chill for 1 hour before serving on a bed of lettuce.

YIELD: 4 SERVINGS

Squash & Brie Quesadillas

A quesadilla is a flour tortilla that is folded around a filling or 2 tortillas that lie flat and work the filling in between. Quesadillas are baked and served with plenty of salsa. Brie makes a rich, luscious cheese filling and the apple, onion, and winter squash add crunchiness and sweetness to the dish. Serve as an appetizer or as a light meal with a tossed salad or bowl of soup.

2 tablespoons butter
2 cups peeled and diced butternut or
   acorn squash
1 green pepper, seeded and diced
½ cup diced red onion
½ cup diced apple
2 jalapeño peppers, seeded and minced

1 cup corn kernels, fresh, canned, or
   frozen and thawed
1 teaspoon ground cumin
1 teaspoon red hot sauce
4 (10-inch) flour tortillas
1 pound brie cheese, crust removed and
   chopped
1½ cups Raspberry Salsa (page 7) or
   Red Tomato Salsa (page 3)
1 cup sour cream

Preheat the oven to 350° F.

In a large skillet, melt the butter and add the squash. Sauté for 4 to 5 minutes. Add the green pepper, onion, apple, and jalapeño peppers; continue to cook for 5 minutes, stirring occasionally. Add the corn, cumin, and red hot sauce; cook for 1 minute longer and then remove from the heat.

Place 2 tortillas on a greased baking sheet. Spread ½ pound of brie on each tortilla. Pour the squash mixture over the brie and spread the mixture evenly to the edges of the tortilla. Cover with the remaining tortillas and place the quesadillas in the oven. Bake for 5 to 7 minutes or until the brie melts.

Place the quesadillas on large round plates and cut each into 4 wedges. Serve immediately with the salsa and sour cream.

YIELD: 4 TO 8 APPETIZER SERVINGS

Blackened Catfish Salad

❖❖

"Blackened" refers to the Cajun practice of heavily spicing and searing fish over extremely high heat. The fish remains moist on the inside and crunchy and spicy on the outside. The blackening technique swept through the country in the eighties, but many cooks overspiced or charred the fish, blackening its reputation. The fiery seasonings should not dominate the fish, but should slide across the taste buds and allow the true flavor of the fish to surface. Although blackened fish is traditionally done in a sauté pan, grilling imbues a smoky flavor and works just as well.

1 head leaf lettuce, torn
1 carrot, shredded
1 red onion, thinly sliced
1 tomato, cut into 6 wedges
4 ounces alfalfa sprouts
1 small jicama, peeled and shredded
8 mushrooms, sliced
1 cup Dijon-Style Mustard Vinaigrette
   (page 165) or a store-bought
   vinaigrette
2 tablespoons Blackened Seasonings
   (page 167) or store-bought Cajun
   seasonings
1½ pounds catfish fillets
4 tablespoons melted butter
1 lemon, quartered
2 cups Corn & Black Bean Salsa
   (page 8); Tomatillo Salsa (page 4);
   or Pineapple-Kiwi Salsa (page 6)

✧✧

Preheat the grill until the coals are gray to white. Meanwhile, arrange the leaf lettuce in the center of 4 round plates. In a circular fashion, place the carrot, onion, tomato, sprouts, jicama, and mushrooms in small piles around the lettuce. Shake the vinaigrette over the greens and vegetables.

When you are ready to grill, lightly sprinkle the Blackened Seasonings over the catfish fillets; place them on the grill. Baste the fillets with half of the butter, but be cautious of a flare-up.

Cook the catfish for 5 to 7 minutes on each side, basting with the remaining butter after turning, and sprinkle more seasonings over the fish. When the catfish is done (white in the center), place the fillets on top of the salads, squeeze a lemon wedge over each fish, and serve at once. Pass the salsa at the table.

The catfish can also be prepared in a sauté pan. Cover the catfish with the Blackened Seasonings, place in a sauté pan, and add 2 tablespoons of melted butter. Cook over medium heat for 5 to 7 minutes and flip.

Sprinkle more Blackened Seasonings over the fish as they cook if you desire a spicier meal.

YIELD: 4 SERVINGS

Chicken Fajita Salad

✧✧

Fajita is a Tex-Mex staple that is usually a buffet of marinated beef or poultry, salsa, cheese, sour cream, and grilled onions and green peppers. It evolved from efforts to make tough, flavorless cuts of beef like skirt steak more palatable. The ingredients vary from region to region, but most marinades include lime juice and garlic. This version makes a nice summer meal with plenty of fresh leaf lettuce and vegetables and can be eaten as a salad or stuffed into a tortilla.

Marinade
1 cup lime juice
1½ cups vegetable oil
½ cup Worcestershire sauce
8 garlic cloves, minced

1 tablespoon dried oregano
1 teaspoon black pepper
1 teaspoon red hot sauce
½ teaspoon salt
2 teaspoons honey

Fajita
2 pounds boneless, skinless chicken
  breasts, cut into 2-inch-wide strips
1 head leaf lettuce, torn
1 cup Dijon-Style Mustard Vinaigrette
  (page 165) or store-bought
  vinaigrette
1 tomato, cut into 8 wedges
2 cups shredded Monterey jack cheese
2 green peppers, seeded and cut into
  strips

✧✧

2 onions, cut into ¼-inch slivers
1 avocado, peeled and quartered
1 large carrot, shredded
4 to 6 (6-inch) flour tortillas (optional)
2 cups Red Tomato Salsa (page 3)

Whisk together all the marinade ingredients. Place the chicken strips in the marinade and refrigerate for at least 3 hours.

Preheat the grill until the coals are gray to white. Meanwhile, mound the leaf lettuce on 4 dinner plates and sprinkle the vinaigrette over. Arrange the tomato, cheese, green peppers, onions, avocado, and carrot around the circumference.

When you are ready to grill, remove the chicken strips from the marinade and drain them. Place them on the grill and cook for 3 to 5 minutes and then turn over. Continue cooking until the strips are white in the center.

Place the grilled chicken on top of the greens. Crisp the flour tortillas by briefly throwing them on the grill and flipping them after a few seconds. Serve the tortillas along with the salad. Pass the salsa at the table.

To eat, fill the flour tortillas with the salad ingredients and salsa, and roll it up like a burrito, or skip the tortilla and enjoy the chicken and vegetables as a salad, passing the extra salsa at the table.

YIELD: 4 SERVINGS

Fiesta Chicken Tortillas

❖❖❖

This is a healthy collection of chicken, vegetables, black beans, and cheese cooked together and wrapped in a tortilla. Shrimp, scallops, crabmeat, or diced pork can be used in place of the chicken for an equally satisfying meal.

1 medium-size sweet potato, diced
  (do not peel)
2 tablespoons butter
1½ pounds boneless and skinless
  chicken breast, diced
1 large green pepper, seeded and diced
1 tomato, diced
8 mushrooms, sliced
½ cup corn kernels, fresh, canned,
  or frozen and thawed

½ cup cooked black beans (page 169)
1 tablespoon ground cumin
2 cups shredded Monterey jack or
  provolone cheese
2 (10-inch) flour tortillas or 4
  (6-inch) flour tortillas, warmed
1 cup Tomatillo Salsa (page 4)
  or Red Tomato Salsa (page 3)
1 cup Papaya Guacamole (page 166)
  or traditional guacamole

Place the sweet potatoes in boiling water to cover and cook for 8 to 10 minutes, or until soft but not mushy. Drain and chill under cold running water.

In a large sauté pan, melt the butter over moderately high heat and add the chicken

✥✥

and green peppers. Cook for 4 to 6 minutes, stirring occasionally. Add the sweet potatoes, tomato, and mushrooms and continue cooking until the chicken is white in the center.

Stir in the corn, black beans, and cumin and bring to a simmer. Reduce the heat to medium and mix in the cheese. As soon as the cheese is melted, pour the mixture into the center of the tortillas, forming a log. Roll the tortillas around the mixture like a burrito. Serve immediately. Pass the salsa and guacamole at the table.

YIELD: 4 APPETIZER OR 2 DINNER SERVINGS

Jay's Café Veggie Tortillas

❖❖

The Moosewood Cookbook has inspired legions of cooks across the country to experiment with vegetarian cuisine. I have a more practical incentive: the Moosewood Restaurant is located around the corner from my restaurant in Ithaca, New York, and it has set a high standard for healthy, vegetarian meals. The Veggie Tortilla, a colorful melange of vegetables and cheese served like a burrito, has become the most popular dish on my menu.

6 broccoli florets
1 tablespoon butter, melted
1 small zucchini, diced
6 mushrooms, sliced
6 cherry tomatoes, halved, or 1 tomato, diced

1 green pepper, diced
1 teaspoon minced jalapeño peppers (optional)
½ cup corn kernels, fresh, canned, or frozen and thawed
2 teaspoons ground cumin
1½ cups shredded Monterey jack cheese
2 (10-inch) flour tortillas, warmed
2 cups Red Tomato Salsa (page 3) or Corn & Black Bean Salsa (page 8)

Blanch the broccoli in boiling water to cover for 3 minutes. Drain and chill under cold running water.

In a large sauté pan, melt the butter. Add the zucchini, mushrooms, tomatoes, pepper, and jalapeños. Sauté over medium heat for about 5 minutes, until all of the vege-

✧✧✧

tables are soft. Reduce the heat and stir in the broccoli, corn, cumin, and cheese. Cook until the cheese melts, about 30 seconds. Remove the pan from the heat.

Place the tortillas on round plates and pour the vegetable and cheese into the center of the tortillas, forming a log. Wrap the tortillas around the vegetable mixture like a burrito or crêpe. Place seam side down on a serving plate and spoon generous portions of the salsa next to the tortilla.

YIELD: 4 APPETIZER OR 2 DINNER SERVINGS

Midnight Omelet

✥✥✥

This omelet was conceived during a midnight raid on the refrigerator. Some of my most innovative dishes have occurred during a hunger rampage. For a hearty breakfast or brunch, serve it with Scallion-Pepper Corn Bread (page 124) and Roasted Garlic Potatoes (page 128).

½ cup cooked black beans (page 169)
½ cup corn kernels, fresh, canned, or
　　frozen and thawed
½ cup minced red or green bell peppers
1 jalapeño pepper, seeded and minced
1 teaspoon red hot sauce
¼ teaspoon cayenne pepper
¼ teaspoon salt
8 eggs, beaten

¼ cup light cream
2 tablespoons butter
1 cup shredded Monterey jack cheese
1 cup Red Tomato Salsa (page 3)
1 cup Papaya Guacamole (page 166)
　　or traditional guacamole

Combine the black beans, corn, bell peppers, jalapeño pepper, red hot sauce, cayenne pepper, and salt in a mixing bowl. Set aside.

Whisk the eggs with the light cream. Melt 1 tablespoon of the butter in an 8-inch omelet pan or well-seasoned skillet. Cook over moderately high heat for about 30 seconds or until the butter is sizzling. Add about ½ cup of the eggs to the pan. Swirl to the edges of the pan. Cook for 1 to 2 minutes; then slide a spatula underneath the omelet to ease the excess mixture onto the pan's surface.

When the omelet is light brown around the edge and the top surface is barely moist, add ⅓ cup of the black bean mixture to one half of the omelet, forming a half moon. Add ¼ cup of the shredded cheese on top of the black bean mixture and gently fold the other half of the omelet over the mixture. Cover the pan, reduce the heat, cook for 15 seconds longer, and then turn the heat off. Let the omelet sit in the pan for 30 seconds and then slide to a warm plate and cover.

Repeat the process with the remaining ingredients. Melt 1 to 2 teaspoons of butter in the pan before cooking each of the remaining omelets.

Serve the omelets with the salsa and guacamole.

YIELD: 4 SERVINGS

Shrimp Pesto Tortillas

❖❖

It is difficult to select a single dish that best exemplifies my cooking philosophy, but the Shrimp Pesto Tortillas comes close. It is an assortment of fresh, crisp, colorful vegetables, combined with shrimp (or chicken) and distinctive seasonings and ingredients (in this case, cashew pesto), and served with a strong, palate-cleansing condiment. Best of all, it is easy to prepare. I like to serve this meal by candlelight, accompanied by a bottle of Chardonnay.

5 to 6 broccoli florets
2 tablespoons butter
1 green pepper, seeded and diced
1 small zucchini, diced
6 mushrooms, sliced
1 tomato, diced
20 to 24 small shrimp, peeled
¼ cup corn kernels, fresh, canned,
    or frozen and thawed
1½ teaspoons ground cumin
¾ cup Cashew Pesto (page 164) or
    commercial or homemade basil pesto
½ cup shredded Monterey jack cheese
2 (12-inch) flour tortillas or 4 (6-inch)
    flour tortillas
2 cups Red Tomato Salsa (page 3)
    or Raspberry Salsa (page 7)

Blanch the broccoli in boiling water to cover for 3 minutes. Drain and chill under cold running water.

Melt the butter in a large skillet. Add the green pepper, zucchini, mushrooms, and tomato. Sauté over medium heat for about 3 minutes, until the vegetables are slightly cooked. Add the broccoli and shrimp and continue cooking until the shrimp are firm and fully cooked, about 7 minutes, stirring occasionally.

Add the corn and cumin; cook for 1 minute more. Add the pesto and cheese and stir all of the ingredients together. Remove the pan from the heat as soon as the cheese and pesto melt.

Place the tortillas on dinner plates and pour the shrimp and pesto mixture into the center. Roll the tortillas around the mixture, forming a log. Serve immediately with the salsa spooned onto the plate next to the tortilla. Rice makes a good accompaniment if you are serving this as a main course.

YIELD: 4 APPETIZER OR 2 DINNER SERVINGS

Cumin-Grilled Salmon

❖❖

There is a variety of salmon found in both the Atlantic and Pacific oceans. Sockeye, pink, chinook, and coho (also known as silver) salmon are harvested in the Pacific Ocean, while Atlantic salmon are primarily farm-raised and imported from Norway and Canada. The larger fish are cut into cross sections and served as steaks, while the smaller fish are served whole, dressed and deboned. I prefer baby coho salmon, which is similar in appearance to rainbow trout; it cooks fast and usually has few bones. Rainbow trout and coho salmon are interchangeable in most of my recipes. The delicate flavor of salmon is complemented by light, citrusy condiments like Pineapple-Kiwi Salsa or Papaya-Tomatillo Salsa. The fish can be grilled or panfried.

4 (8-ounce) coho salmon or rainbow
    trout, dressed and deboned
2 tablespoons melted butter
1 tablespoon ground cumin
1 lime or lemon, quartered
3 cups Pineapple-Kiwi Salsa (page 6) or
    Papaya-Tomatillo Salsa (page 5)

Preheat the grill until the coals are gray to white.

Open the salmon and lightly baste the flesh with the butter. Lay the fish flesh side down on an oiled grill.

After 1 minute, use a spatula to loosen the salmon from the grill to prevent sticking. Flip the salmon after 3 or 4 minutes and cook the skin side just long enough to crisp it, about 2 minutes. Sprinkle cumin lightly over the flesh side while the skin side cooks.

Flip the flesh side back on the grill and finish cooking until the salmon is light pink in the center.

To panfry the fish, heat the 2 tablespoons of butter over moderately high heat in a sauté pan and lay the salmon in the pan flesh side down. Flip after 4 to 5 minutes and sprinkle cumin over the flesh. Flip again and continue cooking until the flesh is light pink in the center.

Remove the salmon to 4 warm plates. Squeeze a wedge of lime over each fish and serve with the salsa.

YIELD: 4 SERVINGS

Lobster & Blue Corn Tacos

Like opening a bottle of wine at table side, there is a certain etiquette associated with eating a lobster. The claws and tail must be properly shucked to extract the most meat, while making the least mess. When I'm done eating a lobster, however, there are shells and spilled butter everywhere. It is an epicurean pillage, a gustatory carnage.

The lobster taco, on the other hand, allows me to indulge in lobster without embarrassment. It turns an ordinary taco meal into a gourmet feast. The ingredients should be served buffet-style, allowing everyone to fill their own taco. You won't need a lobster bib for this meal. It makes a great appetizer or light summer dinner when lobsters are plentiful.

2 (1-pound) live lobsters
1½ cups Tomatillo Salsa (page 4) or Red Tomato Salsa (page 3)
1½ cups Papaya Guacamole (page 166) or traditional guacamole
1½ cups shredded Monterey jack cheese
½ cup minced red onion
½ cup corn kernels, fresh, canned, or frozen and thawed
½ cup cooked black beans (page 169)
4 jalapeño peppers, seeded and minced
4 to 6 leaves leaf lettuce, torn
4 to 6 (6-inch) blue corn tortillas, warmed

❖❖

Place the lobsters in boiling water to cover and cook for 10 to 12 minutes. Drain and let cool for 5 minutes. Remove the lobster meat from the tail and claws and discard the shells (or use to make soup stock). Dice the meat and place in a serving bowl.

Place the salsa, guacamole, cheese, onion, corn, beans, peppers, and lettuce in serving bowls and arrange buffet-style with the lobster and tortillas.

YIELD: 4 TO 6 SERVINGS

Sweet Potato Pancakes

❖❖❖

This is one of those recipes that never looks quite right until it's finished, so stay with it.

2 cups grated raw sweet potatoes
   (do not peel)
3 eggs, beaten
½ cup milk
1 cup cooked black beans (page 169),
   pureed
¼ cup minced red onion
2 tablespoons all-purpose flour
¼ teaspoon salt
⅛ teaspoon black pepper
⅛ teaspoon cayenne pepper
1 tablespoon butter
1 cup Red Tomato Salsa (page 3)
1 cup sour cream

Combine the potatoes, eggs, milk, beans, onion, flour, salt, and peppers; mix well.

Melt the butter over medium heat and ladle ½ cup of the mixture into the pan. Spread out to form a pancake. Flip after 3 minutes, or when the pancake is brown around the edge. Cook the other side until brown. Repeat with the remaining batter. Melt 1 to 2 teaspoons of butter in the pan before cooking each one. Cover the finished pancakes with waxed paper to keep them warm. Serve with the salsa and sour cream.

YIELD: 2 TO 3 SERVINGS

2
Mayonnaises & Mustards

✛✛✛

At the age of 24, I opened up a gourmet sandwich shop. The place had only 6 tables, so I relied heavily on carry-out lunches for my business. One of the things I learned, aside from how to make, cut, and wrap a sandwich in 15 seconds flat, was that there are 2 basic types of customers: those who prefer mayonnaise and those who prefer mustard. Rarely did anyone omit both mayonnaise *and* mustard, nor did they ever switch sides, or use the two together.

The marketing of commercial mayonnaise and mustard has defined (and limited) how we use them. Spread store-bought mayonnaise or mustard over a slab of bread, add some sliced cold meat, maybe a soggy leaf of lettuce, and serve it up with chips. Welcome to lunch time in America.

Walk down the mayonnaise aisle in the grocery store and you'll be greeted by a legion of uniform products. Except for a few low-caloried or no-cholesterol versions, they are for the most part a homogeneous collection of mayonnaises. The Henry Ford philosophy of marketing seems to apply to commercially prepared mayonnaise: you can have any kind you want, just as long as it's plain.

In the world of homemade mayonnaises, the choice of flavor is entirely up to you. With the advent of the food processor, it is possible to make a variety of mayonnaises at home, without spending a lot of effort or time. Crack an egg, add the lemon juice and mustard, process for a few seconds, drizzle in the oil while the motor is running, and presto, you've made mayonnaise! Even if you whisk it by hand, it only takes a few minutes.

Once you've made the basic mayonnaise, it's easy to incorporate a variety of flavors. Adding fresh herbs, such as tarragon, dill, basil, cilantro, or mint, is one of the simplest ways to enhance a homemade mayonnaise. When fresh herbs are not available or when you want a stronger-flavored mayonnaise, try adding jalapeño peppers, horseradish, ginger, garlic, or the zest of a lemon or lime.

A mayonnaise infused with bold new flavors becomes more than a luxurious sandwich spread. Spoon flavored mayonnaises over grilled fish or chicken or sautéed scallops or shrimp. Make your chicken, shrimp, or tuna salads with homemade mayonnaise, and see what a difference it makes. It also adds a rich, smooth dimension to pasta salad and cole slaw.

Most homemade mayonnaises will keep for about 5 days if kept well chilled. If a mayonnaise separates (it may mean that you added the oil too quickly when you were making it), gradually whisk in an egg yolk until it reaches the proper consistency.

The story of mustard is a food trivia buff's dream. Mustard, in the form of a seed, powder, or paste, has been around for thousands of years. The Chinese first combined crushed mustard seeds with cold water to form a fiery paste. Hippocrates and Pythagoras recommended mustard for medicinal purposes, and the Romans carried mustard seeds with them throughout Europe. The Romans, by the way, are thought to have been the first to add sour grape juice (also known as must) to ground mustard seeds. Mustard is alluded to by the Bible and Shakespeare. Around the 18th century, the French started adding unfermented wine (also known as must) to the crushed seed. In America, mustard became associated with hot dogs and hamburgers thanks to the ravenous appetite of sports fans and ball players like Babe Ruth, who was known to consume dozens of hot dogs dripping with mustard at one sitting.

Ten years ago, mustard was still primarily used for sandwiches, hot dogs, and soft pretzels. Dijon-style mustard was considered an esoteric ingredient. As trends veered toward more highly seasoned foods, cooks began using sharp, piquant mustards in sauces, salad dressings, and soups. Lately, Dijon-style mustard has become *de rigueur* in most kitchens.

Mustard is derived from the seeds of the mustard plant; the two most common seeds are white (or yellow) and brown seeds. The seeds by themselves are deceivingly tame. Once they are crushed and mixed with water or another liquid to form a paste, they release a powerful, nose-tingling sensation. A small amount of turmeric gives mustard its familiar bright yellow color.

Mustard sauces make a versatile accompaniment to chicken, pork, soy-marinated beef, and fish. A good mustard sauce strikes a balance between imparting a strong flavor and overpowering the dish. Mustard sauces can be made from a quality prepared mustard or a homemade mustard.

Homemade mustard is usually more potent than its commercial counterpart. As with mayonnaise, the opportunities for this pungent condiment will greatly expand once you break out of the habit of relying on store-bought condiments.

Basic Mayonnaise

I was under a great deal of pressure the first time I ever made mayonnaise. I was serving a sandwich buffet for 50 people, and moments before the group was due to arrive, I realized there was no mayonnaise in the pantry. With no time to run to the store, I found a recipe for homemade mayonnaise, followed the directions without panicking, and made enough mayonnaise for the buffet. Not only was it fast and easy to make, it was far superior to any mayonnaise I could find in a store.

3 egg yolks
1½ tablespoons Dijon-style mustard
¼ cup lemon juice
⅛ teaspoon salt
⅛ teaspoon white pepper
1½ cups olive or vegetable oil

Blend the egg yolks for about 15 seconds in a food processor fitted with a steel blade. Scrape the sides, add the mustard, lemon juice, and seasonings and process for another 10 seconds.

Slowly drizzle in the oil while the motor is running. When half of the oil is left, stop the processor and scrape the sides; then continue processing and drizzling.

Scrape the mayonnaise into a bowl, wrap tightly, and chill. If refrigerated, this mayonnaise should keep for about 5 days.

YIELD: 2 CUPS

Spinach-Dill Mayonnaise

✧✧

Take fresh spinach and dill and suspend them in mayonnaise and you have a condiment the color of an evergreen forest. For an impressive sandwich, spread Spinach-Dill Mayonnaise on dark bread, add roast beef or turkey, tomato, red onion, shredded carrot and lettuce, and garnish with a stem of fresh dill weed.

3 egg yolks
1½ tablespoons Dijon-style mustard
¼ cup lemon juice
3 tablespoons minced fresh dill weed
¼ teaspoon salt
¼ teaspoon black pepper
1½ cups olive or other vegetable oil
3 cups coarsely chopped fresh spinach leaves

Blend the egg yolks for 15 seconds in a food processor fitted with a steel blade. Scrape the sides, add the mustard, lemon juice, dill, and seasonings; process for another 10 seconds.

Slowly drizzle in the oil while the motor is running. When half of the oil is left, stop the processor and scrape the sides; then continue processing and drizzling. Add the spinach and process for another 15 seconds or until the spinach is fully incorporated into the mayonnaise.

Scrape the mayonnaise into a bowl, wrap tightly, and chill. If refrigerated, the mayonnaise should keep for about 5 days.

YIELD: 2 CUPS

Tropical Mayonnaise

✢✢

Serve this light and citrusy mayonnaise with mahimahi, blue marlin, or swordfish, or in a salad with fruity or nutty ingredients, such as pineapple, almonds, apple, coconut, papaya, and avocado.

2 egg yolks
1 tablespoon Dijon-style mustard
2 tablespoons pineapple juice
½ cup olive or other vegetable oil
½ cup coconut milk (see page 151)
¼ cup shredded fresh coconut or
  unsweetened dried coconut
¼ teaspoon salt
¼ teaspoon white pepper
1 tablespoon grated orange zest

Blend the egg yolks for 15 seconds in a food processor fitted with a steel blade. Scrape the sides and add the mustard and pineapple juice and process for another 10 seconds.

Slowly drizzle in the oil while the motor is running. When half of the oil is left, stop the processor and scrape the sides; then continue processing and drizzling. Add the coconut milk, coconut, salt, pepper, and orange zest and process for another 10 seconds.

Scrape the mayonnaise into a bowl, wrap tightly, and chill. If refrigerated, the mayonnaise should keep for about 4 days.

YIELD: 1 CUP

Jalapeño-Pimento Mayonnaise

❖❖❖

Sweet pimentos combine with fiery jalapeño peppers to form an exotic fuchsia-colored mayonnaise. For a spicier mayonnaise, add the jalapeño seeds as well.

3 egg yolks
1½ tablespoons Dijon-style mustard
¼ cup lemon or lime juice
¼ teaspoon white pepper
⅛ teaspoon cayenne pepper
⅛ teaspoon salt
1 teaspoon red hot sauce
1½ cups olive or other vegetable oil
6 jalapeño peppers, seeded and minced
½ cup canned whole pimentos, drained
    and diced
1 tablespoon dried chives

Blend the egg yolks for 15 seconds in a food processor fitted with a steel blade. Add the mustard, lemon juice, and seasonings and process for another 15 seconds.

Slowly drizzle the oil into the mixture while the motor is running. When half of the oil is left, stop the processor and scrape the sides; then continue processing and drizzling. Add the jalapeño peppers and pimentos to the mixture and process for another 10 seconds.

Scrape the mayonnaise into a bowl and fold in the chives. Wrap tightly and chill for at least 1 hour. If refrigerated, the mayonnaise should keep for about 5 days.

YIELD: 2¼ CUPS

Feisty Almond Mayonnaise

✧✧✧

This mayonnaise is especially good with roast beef, prime rib, and T-bone steaks. If fresh horseradish is unavailable, prepared horseradish can be substituted.

3 egg yolks
1½ tablespoons Dijon-style mustard
¼ cup lemon juice
1½ cups olive or other vegetable oil
¾ cup minced fresh horseradish (or ½ cup prepared horseradish)
1 cup slivered blanched almonds
1 teaspoon almond extract
½ teaspoon white pepper
¼ teaspoon salt

Blend the egg yolks for 15 seconds in a food processor fitted with a steel blade. Scrape the sides and add the mustard and lemon juice; process for another 10 seconds.

Slowly drizzle in the oil while the motor is running. When half of the oil is left, stop the processor and scrape the sides; then continue processing and drizzling. Add the horseradish, almonds, almond extract, pepper, and salt and process for another 10 seconds.

Scrape the mayonnaise into a bowl, wrap tightly, and chill. If refrigerated, the mayonnaise should keep for about 5 days.

YIELD: 3 CUPS

Wasabi-Ginger Mayonnaise

Known as Japanese horseradish, wasabi is a green powder that is mixed with water to form a potent paste. Its penetrating flavor is best appreciated when it is combined with other ingredients, in this case ginger and lime.

2½ tablespoons wasabi (available where Oriental foods are sold)
2½ tablespoons water
3 egg yolks
¼ cup lime juice
1½ tablespoons Dijon-style mustard
1½ tablespoons minced fresh parsley
2 tablespoons minced fresh ginger root
¼ teaspoon salt
⅛ teaspoon cayenne pepper
¼ teaspoon red hot sauce
1½ cups olive or other vegetable oil

Mix the wasabi and water together to form a paste. Let stand for 5 minutes.

Blend the egg yolks for 15 seconds in a food processor. Scrape the sides; add the lime juice, mustard, parsley, ginger, seasonings, and wasabi. Process for 20 seconds, stopping to scrape the sides at least once. Slowly drizzle in the oil. When half is left, scrape the sides; then continue processing and drizzling.

Scrape the mayonnaise into a bowl, wrap tightly, and chill. If refrigerated, the mayonnaise should keep for about 5 days.

YIELD: 2 CUPS

Pesto Mayonnaise

✛✛

Pesto is an earthy blend of fresh basil, garlic, nuts, cheese, and olive oil. The ingredients are pureed together to form a potent, aromatic paste. The aroma of basil lingers on your fingers when you are preparing it and is as strong and distinctive as the scent of a rose. Pesto mayonnaise can be used as a spread for sandwiches, a sauce for seafood or chicken, or as a dip for crudités.

3 egg yolks
1½ tablespoons Dijon-style mustard
¼ cup lemon juice
⅛ teaspoon salt
⅛ teaspoon black pepper
1½ cups olive oil
1 cup Cashew Pesto (page 164) or
    commercial or homemade pesto

Blend the egg yolks for 15 seconds in a food processor fitted with a steel blade. Scrape the sides and add the mustard, lemon juice, and seasonings; process for another 10 seconds.

Slowly drizzle in the oil while the motor is running. When half of the oil is left, stop the processor and scrape the sides; then continue processing and drizzling. Add the pesto and process for 10 to 15 seconds, until the pesto is fully incorporated.

Serve immediately or wrap tightly and chill. If refrigerated, the mayonnaise should keep for at least 5 days.

YIELD: 3 CUPS

Basil Aioli

✧✧

Aioli, a classic French sauce, is a rich, creamy mayonnaise with the divine redolence of garlic lingering throughout. Fresh basil adds another dimension to the traditional French version. If fresh basil is unavailable, substitute 1½ cups of fresh spinach.

1 egg yolk
1 teaspoon Dijon-style mustard
2 tablespoons lemon juice
¼ teaspoon white pepper
⅛ teaspoon cayenne pepper
⅛ teaspoon salt
¾ cup olive oil
½ cup loosely packed basil leaves
6 to 8 garlic cloves, minced

Blend the egg yolks for 15 seconds in a food processor fitted with a steel blade. Scrape the sides and add the mustard, lemon juice, and seasonings; then process for another 10 seconds.

Slowly drizzle in the oil while the motor is running. When half of the oil is left, stop the processor and scrape the sides; then continue processing and drizzling. Add the basil and garlic and process for another 15 seconds, or until the ingredients are fully incorporated.

Scrape the aioli into a bowl, wrap tightly, and chill. If refrigerated, the aioli should keep for about 5 days.

YIELD: 1 CUP

Basic Mustard

✛✛

I have found that most recipes for mustard are too salty or too pungent. This version is a kinder, gentler mustard. It is strong but not too overbearing.

½ cup dry mustard
2½ tablespoons all-purpose flour
2 tablespoons brown sugar
¼ teaspoon salt
½ cup white wine vinegar

Combine the dry mustard, flour, sugar, and salt in a mixing bowl and blend well. Gradually stir the vinegar into the mixture, forming a smooth paste. Cover the mustard and refrigerate for at least 2 hours before serving. If kept refrigerated, the mustard should keep for several weeks.

YIELD: ABOUT 1 CUP

Variation:
Herb Mustard. Add 1 teaspoon each of fresh minced basil, tarragon, and chives (fresh marjoram, mint, or dill weed may be substituted for any of the herbs).

Champagne Honey Mustard

‡‡

This mustard is smooth, but with a sweet and hot bite to it. Like most mustards, its potency is somewhat diminished after a day or two in the refrigerator. If you prefer a milder mustard, make it a day ahead of time.

½ cup dry mustard
2 tablespoons all-purpose flour
¼ teaspoon salt
¼ cup champagne
¼ white wine vinegar
½ cup honey
1 egg, beaten

Combine the dry mustard, flour, and salt in the top of a double boiler. Gradually whisk in the champagne, vinegar, honey, and egg to form a smooth paste. Cook over simmering water for about 10 minutes, stirring occasionally.

Serve the mustard immediately or wrap and refrigerate. In the refrigerator, the mustard will keep for about 1 week.

YIELD: ABOUT 1 CUP

Apple-Pear Mustard

+++

Of all the fiery spices that I have encountered, dry mustard powder (or seed) is one of the most difficult to tame. Its potent, sharp flavor easily overpowers a dish if it is not harnessed. I have found that apples and pears temper the mustard flavor.

¼ cup yellow mustard seeds
¼ cup white wine
5 tablespoons apple cider vinegar
¼ cup water
½ cup diced apple (do not peel)
½ cup diced pear (do not peel)
1 tablespoon minced shallot
2 tablespoons brown sugar
½ teaspoon white pepper
½ teaspoon salt
1 teaspoon all-purpose flour

Combine the mustard seeds, white wine, 4 tablespoons of the vinegar, the apple, pear, shallots, sugar, pepper, and salt in a saucepan. Simmer over medium heat, stirring occasionally, for 8 to 10 minutes, or until the liquid is reduced by half.

Place the mixture in a blender and add the remaining 1 tablespoon vinegar and the flour. Blend on high speed for 20 to 30 seconds, or until the mustard forms a thick, coarse paste.

Serve immediately or wrap and chill. If refrigerated, the mustard should keep for about 2 weeks.

YIELD: ¾ CUP

Mustard Cream Sauce

This is a simple sauce with myriad applications. It only takes a few seconds to blend, and it can be stored for at least a week in the refrigerator. Serve it with grilled beef, chicken, pork, and fish, and dishes with soy-based marinades or sauces. It is important to use a quality mustard to achieve the best results.

¾ cup light or heavy cream
¼ cup Dijon-style mustard
(or Champagne Honey Mustard,
page 42)
⅛ teaspoon white pepper

Combine all of the ingredients in a small bowl and chill.

For dishes that require a warmed mustard sauce, microwave the sauce until it simmers or place it on top of a double boiler and bring it to the desired temperature.

YIELD: 1 CUP

Variations:
Jalapeño Mustard Sauce. Add 2 jalapeño peppers, seeded and minced.
Mint Mustard Sauce. Add ¼ cup minced mint leaves.
Tarragon Mustard Sauce. Add 1 tablespoon dried tarragon.

Pork Chops with Mustard

✚✚✚

This is an easy and tasty way to prepare pork chops. Flambéing the dish is not crucial, but adds an elegant touch. When you are using spirits to flambé anything, never pour the liquor directly from the bottle to the pan. It is much safer to pour it from a cup.

2 tablespoons butter
4 (6-ounce) pork chops, boneless and
   butterflied
3 apples, sliced (do not peel)
¼ cup brandy
1½ cups Apple-Pear Mustard (page 43)
½ cup heavy cream
¼ cup minced fresh mint

Melt the butter in a sauté pan and add the pork chops. Cook the pork over moderate heat for 4 to 5 minutes, and then turn and cook the other side. After about 3 minutes, add the apple slices and brandy to the pan. Remove the pan from the heat. Ignite the brandy with a long kitchen match. Flambé until the flames are extinguished. Then continue cooking for another 2 minutes, or until the pork is white in the center.

Remove the pork chops to warm plates. Add the Apple-Pear Mustard and heavy cream to the apple slices and pan juices. Bring to a simmer over medium heat. Pour the sauce over the pork chops, sprinkle with fresh mint, and serve immediately.

YIELD: 4 SERVINGS

Janet's Rice & Veggie Sauté

*This is my friend Janet's favorite dish. It's a
healthy collection of vegetables seasoned
with soy sauce, chili-garlic paste, sesame
oil, and lime juice. This dish can easily be
prepared in a wok; simply omit the blanch-
ing of the broccoli and substitute 1 tablespoon of peanut oil for the butter.*

8 broccoli florets
2 tablespoons butter
4 tablespoons soy sauce
1 teaspoon sesame oil
¼ teaspoon hot sesame oil
2 tablespoons lime juice
1½ tablespoons minced fresh ginger
  root

1 to 2 teaspoons chili-garlic paste or red
  curry paste (available where Oriental
  foods are sold)
12 ears canned baby corn
1 red pepper, seeded and diced
6 mushrooms, sliced
1½ inches daikon, thinly sliced
½ cup diced fresh pineapple
2 cups cooked white rice
2 teaspoons minced fresh cilantro
½ cup Mint Mustard Sauce (page 44) or
  Mustard Cream Sauce (page 44)

Blanch the broccoli in boiling water to cover
for 3 minutes; then drain. Chill under cold
running water and set aside.

Melt the butter in a large sauté pan or skillet over medium heat. Add 2 tablespoons of the soy sauce, the sesame oil, hot oil, 1 tablespoon of the lime juice, the ginger, and chili paste and heat until it sizzles. Add the broccoli, baby corn, red pepper, mushrooms, daikon, and pineapple, and cook for 5 to 7 minutes, stirring occasionally.

Add the rice, the remaining 2 tablespoons soy sauce, lime juice, and cilantro, and toss thoroughly. Cook for 2 to 3 minutes longer or until the rice steams.

Remove the mixture to warm plates. Serve immediately with the mustard sauce.

YIELD: 2 DINNER OR 4 SIDE DISH SERVINGS

Polynesian Bluefish

The ability to successfully merchandise a fish often depends upon an appealing nomenclature. Boston bluefish and Atlantic pollock refer to the same fish, but customers are more likely to order Boston bluefish than pollock. Whatever the name, the fish is very tasty and usually inexpensive. Its flaky, white flesh is similar to haddock and codfish. The marinade of pineapple juice, soy sauce, and mirin flavor the fish without overpowering it. This marinade works well with a variety of fish, including haddock, tuna, mahimahi, and swordfish. The fish bakes to a golden hue, and the Mustard Cream Sauce offers a warm, contrasting flavor.

½ cup soy sauce
½ cup pineapple juice
½ cup mirin or sake
2 tablespoons sesame oil
2 tablespoons lime juice
2 teaspoons hot sesame oil
2 teaspoons dried red pepper flakes
2 tablespoons minced fresh ginger root
1½ pounds Boston bluefish or haddock fillets
1 lime, quartered
1 cup Mustard Cream Sauce (page 44), warmed

Combine the soy sauce, pineapple juice, mirin, sesame oil, lime juice, hot oil, red pepper flakes, and ginger in a shallow glass

✤✤

baking dish. Add the fish and marinate in the refrigerator for 2 hours. Turn the fillets after 1 hour.

Preheat the oven to 400° F.

Place the fish on a greased baking pan and pour the excess marinade over the fish. Bake for 12 to 15 minutes, or until the center of the fish is opaque and easily flakes with a fork.

Remove the fish to warm plates and squeeze lime over each portion. Spoon the sauce over the top of each fish. Serve with rice or Herbed Couscous (page 168).

YIELD: 4 SERVINGS

Coconut-Crusted Catfish

✧✧✧

Farm-raised catfish is mildly flavored and firm, ideal for grilling, sautéing, or frying. Catfish benefits by being served with strongly flavored condiments, such as Feisty Almond Mayonnaise, Jalapeño-Pimento Mayonnaise, and Cherry Tomato-Date Catsup. The cornmeal and coconut crust adds a nice nutty crunch.

1 large egg, beaten
1 cup milk
¾ cup yellow cornmeal
¼ cup all-purpose flour
1 teaspoon black pepper
½ teaspoon salt
2 cups grated fresh coconut
2 pounds catfish fillets

2 tablespoons butter
2 tablespoons olive or peanut oil
1 lemon, quartered
2 cups Feisty Almond Mayonnaise
  (page 37)
2 cups Cherry Tomato-Date Catsup
  (page 73)

Preheat the oven to 400° F.

Combine the egg and milk in a shallow dish. Blend the cornmeal, flour, pepper, salt, and coconut in a mixing bowl.

Soak the catfish in the egg and milk mixture and then dredge in the cornmeal and flour, firmly packing the dry ingredients onto the flesh.

In an ovenproof sauté pan, combine the

✿✿

butter and oil and heat over moderately high heat. When the pan is sizzling, add the catfish and cook for 3 to 5 minutes on each side.

Finish in the oven by baking for 7 to 10 minutes, or until the catfish is white in the center.

Squeeze the lemon over the fillets and serve at once with the mayonnaise and catsup.

YIELD: 4 SERVINGS

Wasabi-Grilled Trout

+++

One of the regrets that I have is that when I was growing up I never ever caught a trout. I caught bluegills, sun fish, and rock bass, all of which weren't worth the bait that I hooked them on, but never a prized trout. My brother and cousin were full of riveting fishing stories (and trout 2 feet long to back them up), but I grew frustrated at an early age and gave up. Now that I am older, my revenge is that I have discovered many delectable ways to prepare it. Once in the kitchen, the trout can't elude me.

4 (8-ounce) rainbow trout, dressed and
    deboned
¼ cup melted butter
1 tablespoon paprika

1 cup Wasabi-Ginger Mayonnaise
    (page 38), Basil Aioli (page 40), or
    Pesto Mayonnaise (page 39)
1 lime, quartered

Preheat the grill until the coals are gray to white.

Open the trout and baste the flesh with the melted butter. Lay the trout flesh side down on an oiled grill.

After 1 minute, loosen the trout from the grill to prevent sticking. Flip the trout after 3 or 4 minutes and cook skin side down just long enough to crisp the skin, about 2 minutes. Sprinkle paprika lightly over the trout while the flesh side is up.

Flip the flesh side back onto the grill and

✧✧✧

cook until the trout flesh is clear white in the center.

Remove the trout to warm plates. Spoon about a tablespoon of Wasabi-Ginger Mayonnaise and squeeze a lime wedge over each fish. Pass the extra mayonnaise at the table.

YIELD: 4 SERVINGS

Baked Haddock with Mustard

✛✛✛

Haddock is a flaky, white fish with a delicate flavor. Unfortunately, it is often fried in oil and smothered with tartar sauce so that its flavor is obliterated. A dash of lemon and wine are all it needs. A light, spicy condiment makes a good accompaniment.

1½ pounds haddock fillets
2 tablespoons lemon juice
2 tablespoons dry white wine
2 tablespoons melted butter
1 tablespoon paprika
2 cups Mustard Cream Sauce (page 44),
    Jalapeño-Pimento Mayonnaise (page
    36), or Champagne Honey Mustard,
    (page 42)
1 lemon, quartered

Preheat the oven to 400° F.

Pat the haddock dry and check for bones. Place the haddock on a greased baking pan and spoon the lemon juice, wine, and butter over the fillets. Lightly sprinkle the paprika over the fillets and bake for 10 to 15 minutes, until the center of the fish is clear white and it flakes easily with a fork.

Remove the haddock to warm plates, spoon the condiment and squeeze the lemon over the fish. Serve with rice, Herbed Couscous (page 168), or Roasted Garlic Potatoes (page 128).

YIELD: 4 SERVINGS

Tropical Shrimp Salad

Papayas add a sweet, melon-like flavor to summer salads. Their skin varies from green when they are unripe to yellowish-orange when they are fully ripe. Like an avocado, a papaya should be soft but not mushy when pressed, and free of any blemishes. The inner core of seeds is easily removed and the flesh can be scooped out, leaving the shell intact to serve as a salad bowl.

2 medium-size papayas
24 medium-size shrimp, peeled,
   deveined, and cooked
¾ cup minced celery
½ cup diced fresh pineapple
¼ cup unsweetened shredded coconut
½ cup Tropical Mayonnaise (page 35)
½ teaspoon salt
¼ teaspoon cayenne pepper
1 lime, quartered

Cut the papayas in half lengthwise and scoop out the seeds. Scoop out the pulp but leave the shells in tact. Refrigerate the shells.

Dice the papaya pulp. Combine with the remaining ingredients, except the lime, in a mixing bowl and chill for 1 hour.

Spoon the salad into the papaya shells and squeeze the lime over all. Serve at once.

YIELD: 4 SERVINGS

Scallops with Pesto Mayonnaise

Sometimes I can better judge a meal by washing the dishes at the end of the night than by asking guests in the dining room how everything was. The plates on which I serve Scallops with Pesto Mayonnaise come back scraped clean almost every time I serve it. Guests seem to relish every last morsel.

10 to 12 broccoli florets
2 tablespoons butter
1 pound sea scallops, washed and patted dry
¼ cup dry white wine
1 lemon, quartered
1 cup Pesto Mayonnaise (page 39)

Blanch the broccoli in boiling water to cover for 3 minutes. Drain and chill under cold running water.

Over moderately high heat, melt the butter in a skillet. Add the scallops when the butter is sizzling and cook for 3 to 4 minutes, stirring occasionally. Add the wine and continue to cook for another 3 to 4 minutes, or until the scallops are white in the center and slightly crusty on the outside. Add the blanched broccoli and cook for 1 minute more.

Remove the scallops and broccoli to warm plates, squeeze lemon over each portion, and spoon the Pesto Mayonnaise liberally over the scallops. Serve at once.

YIELD: 3 TO 4 SERVINGS

Sautéed Scallops with Basil Aioli

✛✛✛

My first summer away from home was spent working at a restaurant in Chatham, Massachusetts, on Cape Cod. I became enamored of the beaches, the gentle breeze and salty smell off the ocean, the gazebo in the town square (a marching band played there every Friday night), and, of course, the bounty of fresh seafood, especially the scallops. Scallops are best served with sauces that gently coax out their delicate ocean-raised flavor.

2 tablespoons butter
1 pound sea scallops, washed and
   patted dry
¼ cup dry white wine
1 lemon, quartered
   1 cup Basil Aioli (page 40)

Over moderately high heat, melt the butter in a skillet. When the butter is sizzling, add the scallops and sauté for 3 to 4 minutes. Add the wine and continue to cook the scallops for another 3 to 4 minutes, or until the scallops are white in the center and slightly crusty on the outside.

Remove the scallops to warm plates and squeeze lemon over each portion. Spoon the aioli liberally over the scallops. Serve at once.

YIELD: 3 TO 4 SERVINGS

New York Strip au Poivre

❖❖

Steak au poivre, or peppered steak, refers to the classic French method of smothering a steak in peppercorns. This version offers a triumvirate of flavors: the natural succulence of the beef, the potent zing of the peppercorns, and the velvet pungency of the mustard. Fresh chives lend an elegant touch. I like to wash it all down with a cold, dark beer.

¼ cup black peppercorns, coarsely
   crushed
4 (8-ounce to 10-ounce) boneless strip
   steaks, well trimmed
½ cup Champagne Honey Mustard
   (page 42), warmed
¼ cup light or heavy cream

2 tablespoons butter (for panfried
   version)
¼ cup minced fresh chives

Preheat the grill until the coals are gray to white.

Place the peppercorns in a shallow dish. Firmly press the steaks in the peppercorns, coating both sides.

Combine the mustard and cream in a small bowl and set aside.

Place the steaks on an oiled grill. Cook for 2 to 3 minutes for rare, 3 to 4 minutes for medium rare, 5 to 6 minutes for medium, 7 to 9 minutes for medium well, and for about 10 minutes for well done. Flip the steaks and continue cooking until the steaks reach the desired doneness.

❖❖

To panfry the steaks, melt the butter in a skillet over medium heat. Add the steaks and cook on both sides until the steaks reach the desired doneness.

Remove the steaks to warmed dinner plates and spoon about 2 tablespoons of the sauce over each steak. Sprinkle the chives over the steaks and serve immediately.

YIELD: 4 SERVINGS

Thai-Grilled Beef

✛✛✛

Soy sauce and mustard are two ingredients that naturally complement each other, like tomato and basil and vinegar and oil. In this dish the marinade imparts a strong, soy-ginger flavor to the beef and is wonderfully balanced by the smoothness of the Mustard Cream Sauce. It will melt in your mouth.

1 cup soy sauce
1 cup Worcestershire sauce
1 cup vegetable oil
2 tablespoons minced fresh ginger root
6 to 8 garlic cloves, minced
6 drops red hot sauce or hot oil
1 tablespoon sesame oil
1 tablespoon honey
1 teaspoon black pepper

1 teaspoon dried red pepper flakes
1 orange, quartered
1½ pounds sirloin steak, well trimmed
   and cut ½ inch thick
1½ cups Mustard Cream Sauce (page
   44)

Combine the soy sauce, Worcestershire sauce, oil, ginger, garlic, red hot sauce, sesame oil, honey, and seasonings in a bowl and whisk well. Squeeze the orange sections into the marinade and drop the fruit into the mixture. Chill for at least 1 hour. (This can be done 1 day ahead of time.)

Cut the steak into 2-inch cubes and place the cubes in the chilled marinade for 3 to 4 hours, rearranging and tossing the meat after about 1 hour.

Preheat the grill until the coals are gray to white.

When you are ready to grill the meat, drain the marinated cubes by placing them in a colander. (It is important to drain the meat first, as grilling the cubes straight from the marinade will cause an excessive flare-up.) Discard the marinade.

Place the beef in a row on the grill and use tongs to turn each piece after 2 minutes. Grill each side for 2 to 3 minutes or to desired doneness.

While the marinated beef is grilling, microwave the Mustard Cream Sauce for 20 to 30 seconds, until it is simmering. If you don't have a microwave, heat the sauce over low heat, or in a double boiler over simmering water, stirring frequently, until it begins to simmer. (This can also be done immediately after the beef is removed from the grill.)

Pour the sauce onto warm dinner plates, swirling the plates to form a circle with the sauce. Place the beef cubes on the sauce. Serve with Herbed Couscous (page 168) or rice.

YIELD: 2 TO 3 SERVINGS

Fruity Chicken Salad

✧✧

There is a variety of fruits and nuts that I use to flavor chicken salad: apples, pears, walnuts, slivered almonds, raisins, raspberries, mangoes, and unsalted peanuts. It's important to thoroughly chill the chicken before making the salad, as it will taste fresher and last longer. Take the salad along for an afternoon picnic in the park, and fill the rest of your picnic basket with a loaf of French bread, a wedge of havarti or colby cheese, and a fruity wine cooler.

1 pound cooked chicken breasts,
   diced and chilled
1 cup diced celery
½ pound seedless grapes, halved
¾ cup raw, unsalted cashews

½ cup Basic Mayonnaise (page 33)
¼ cup sour cream
1 tablespoon dried tarragon
¼ teaspoon white pepper
¼ teaspoon black pepper
¼ teaspoon salt

Combine all of the ingredients in a large mixing bowl and toss together thoroughly. Refrigerate for at least 1 hour before serving.

   Serve on a bed of lettuce as a salad or make as a sandwich with lettuce and tomato.

YIELD: 4 TO 6 SERVINGS

Pesto Chicken Salad

✧✧✧

Pesto Mayonnaise, apples, and nuts are natural ingredients for chicken salad. Although any variety of apple will do, I prefer Cortlands, since they don't brown after they've been chopped.

1 pound cooked chicken breasts,
   diced and chilled
1 cup diced celery
1 large apple, cored and diced
   (do not peel)
¾ cup chopped walnuts or pecans
½ cup Pesto Mayonnaise (page 39)
¼ cup sour cream
¼ teaspoon white pepper
¼ teaspoon black pepper
¼ teaspoon salt

Combine all of the ingredients in a large mixing bowl and toss together thoroughly. Refrigerate for at least 1 hour before serving.

Serve on a bed of lettuce as a salad or in a hollowed-out loaf of French bread as a hearty sandwich with lettuce and tomato.

YIELD: 4 TO 6 SERVINGS

Mustard Chicken with Pasta

+‑+

New York State is apple country, and so I incorporate a variety of apples into my meals. Northern spies, greenings, and Ida reds are the best for sautéing, since they are firm and hold up well in a sauce. The Mustard Cream Sauce blends well with the tart apples and crunchy cashews.

8 ounces uncooked linguine
2 tablespoons butter
1½ pounds boneless and skinless chicken breasts, diced
2 apples or pears, sliced (do not peel)
1¼ cups raw, unsalted cashews
2¼ cups Mustard Cream Sauce or any variation (page 44)

Cook the pasta in boiling water to cover according to the package directions, or until just tender, stirring occasionally. Drain and set aside.

In a large skillet, melt the butter over medium heat and add the chicken. Sauté for 5 to 7 minutes. Add the apples and cashews and sauté for 2 to 3 minutes, or until the chicken is white in the center.

Stir the mustard sauce into the pan and bring the mixture to a simmer, still stirring. Cook for about 1 minute more, and then thoroughly blend the pasta into the mixture. Cook for about 1 minute more, or until the pasta is steaming. Serve on warm plates.

YIELD: 4 TO 5 SERVINGS

3
Catsups, Chutneys, & Relishes

✦✦

Vinegar is the hero of this chapter. It is a traditional staple with myriad possibilities. Its strong, tart flavor and preserving capabilities make a variety of condiments possible. Vinegar, which means "soured wine" in French, a liquid that I have great difficulty tasting by itself, has transformed the way I cook.

Catsup is made with vinegar, fruit, onion, and sugar; it is smooth, subtly sweet, and has a slight tang. Most people think of catsup as the ubiquitous tomato condiment commercially produced and mass-marketed and rarely consider it outside the context of their shopping lists. Former President Reagan's administration wanted to classify it as a vegetable for school lunch programs and that caused a lot of people to think about catsup, if only to question whether it was a vegetable or not.

Catsup is not limited to tomatoes, however. There is a variety of fruits, both dried and fresh, that yield wonderful, richly flavored catsups. And catsups are as easy to make as a homemade soup. Discovering homemade catsups may inspire a catsup renaissance in your household. Serve fruity catsups like Apricot-Peach, Rhubarb-Plum, and Cranberry Catsup with roasted pork or chicken. Offer Sun-Dried Tomato Catsup with roast beef, prime rib, or T-bone steaks. And, of course, homemade catsups can beautifully adorn hamburgers, grilled chicken sandwiches, steak fries, and hash browns.

I first learned about chutney at a swank Boston café where I was briefly employed as a manager. Through a trendy haze of purple eggplant and wilting radicchio emerged a genuinely rewarding dish: a chicken breast sandwich topped with Major Grey's chutney. The customers raved about this intriguing combination.

Years later I re-created the dish at my own restaurant, but unable to locate any Major Grey's, I cautiously brewed my first batch of homemade chutney. The result was inspiring. It was a fragrant blend of fruit, onion, and vinegar, accented with ginger, garlic, curry seasonings, and hot spices. Savory and piquant, the condiment imparted varying degrees of sweetness, tartness, and spiciness.

Giving up store-bought condiments to make my own chutney was like entering a new frontier. I was no longer limited to Major Grey's, the generic chutney made from mangoes. Chutney originated as an Indian relish derived from a variety of ingredients, and I merely retraced its roots. Apples, pears, peaches, tomatoes, cranberries, rhubarb, and many other fruits and vegetables produce an abundance of chutneys with wonderful nuances.

Most chutneys are surprisingly easy to make. All of the ingredients, except the ginger and garlic, are coarsely chopped and combined with vinegar and seasonings and simmered. (The ginger and garlic are minced and then added.) After about an hour, the condiment cooks to a jam-like consistency and is transformed into a thick, colorful potion with a rich fragrance. It is also easy to make the chutney hotter, sweeter, or more tart by adjusting the amount of vinegar, sugar, hot seasonings, or fruit.

Most chutneys can be refrigerated for 2 to 3 weeks without losing their potency. Canning is traditionally the way to preserve large batches, since chutney is a vinegar-based condiment and vinegar is a natural preservative (see Notes on Canning, page 172).

You can use chutney in a variety of ways. It adds zest and spice to grilled chicken, seafood, or pork. Spoon chutney over a baked potato, winter squash, or steamed vegetables. Add it to curry dishes, soups, salad dressings, sour cream dips, omelets, or pasta salads. Spread it over dark bread and top it with cheddar or Monterey jack cheese.

While chutney may be a newcomer to your kitchen, relishes are as American as apple pie and chocolate chip cookies. A trip to the ballpark or county fair isn't complete without a hot dog or hamburger topped with pickle relish. Cranberry relish is passed across every table in the country at Thanksgiving. And corn relish is often brought along to another American tradition, the backyard barbecue.

In the past, relishes were a way to preserve surplus fruit and vegetables. The kind of relish available depended on what grew well in the garden that year. If there was an abundance of cucumbers, you made pickle relish. Lots of tomatoes? You made tomato relish. Not much thought was given toward preparing a small batch of relish for one or two meals.

The relishes I enjoy the most can be made in small batches any time of the year and don't need to be canned. I make my favorite relishes with bright, crisp vegetables, combined with dried or fresh fruit. Bananas, beets, jicama, figs, dates, apricots, and nuts are some of the ingredients I use, as well as cranberries, cucumbers, and corn. These relishes have intense colors and flavors and complement a wide variety of marinated fish and chicken, roast pork, game hens, and turkey. Relishes also make tangy toppings for warm vegetables, baked squash or potatoes, and fresh, leafy salads.

Relishes, like chutneys and catsups, are made with vinegar, fruit, vegetables, and sugar. Relishes are usually sweeter than chutneys and catsups, with just a hint of tartness. The flavor of the individual ingredients is more pronounced and less blended. Relishes can be either cooked or uncooked.

Today's busy cooks shouldn't be daunted because they lack a canning basement or the time to undertake a major cooking project. There are a number of condiments in this chapter that are quick and easy to prepare. The only equipment needed is a food processor or blender and a nonreactive, heavy-gauge saucepan. The acid of the vinegar will react with aluminum sauce-pans, causing an off-flavor. These vinegar-based condiments should therefore be cooked in pots of heavy-gauge stainless steel, porcelain-clad cast iron, or other similarly coated materials. Most of the condiments have a refrigerated shelf life of 2 to 3 weeks or can be canned to keep for several months. And most call for ingredients that can be found any time of the year, even in a small town like Ithaca, New York.

Basic Tomato Catsup

❖❖

Firm, ripe tomatoes make the best home-made catsup. This catsup glistens with a bright red hue. If a store-bought catsup could dream, it would dream of becoming this catsup.

3 tomatoes, diced
½ cup diced onion
½ cup red wine vinegar
½ cup canned crushed tomatoes
⅓ cup brown sugar
¼ cup water
½ teaspoon chili powder
½ teaspoon onion powder
½ teaspoon red hot sauce
¼ teaspoon black pepper
¼ teaspoon salt

Combine all of the ingredients in a saucepan and bring to a simmer over medium heat. Simmer for 20 to 25 minutes, stirring occasionally. Remove from the heat and puree in a food processor fitted with a steel blade or in a blender for 30 seconds. The catsup will still be slightly chunky.

Serve immediately or wrap and chill. If refrigerated, the catsup should keep for about 2 weeks.

YIELD: 1½ CUPS

Sun-Dried Tomato Catsup

✤✤

Sun-dried tomatoes yield a dark, robust catsup that is intensely rich with tomato flavor. I prefer to use the dried tomatoes that are packed dry because they are less expensive than the dried tomatoes packed in oil.

3 ounces sun-dried tomatoes
   (about 36 dried tomatoes)
6 cups boiling water
3 fresh tomatoes, diced
6 garlic cloves, minced
¼ cup minced onion
½ cup red wine vinegar
⅓ cup pure maple syrup
1 tablespoon brown sugar
½ teaspoon salt
¼ teaspoon white pepper

Place the dried tomatoes in the boiling water for 2 minutes, drain, and discard the soaking water. (If the tomatoes are packed in oil, you can skip this step.)

Combine all of the ingredients and cook over medium heat for 10 minutes, stirring occasionally. Reduce the heat to low and cook for 3 to 5 minutes, or until the mixture is thick and chunky. Remove from the heat and let stand for 5 minutes. Pour into a food processor or blender and blend for 15 seconds, or until smooth.

Serve the catsup immediately or wrap and chill. If refrigerated, the catsup should keep for about 2 weeks.

YIELD: 2 CUPS

Rhubarb-Plum Catsup

✧✧

One summer in Boston I rode the subway from Harvard Square to Park Street every morning. Upon emerging from the bustling underground station, I (and hundreds of other commuters) was greeted by fresh fruit stands, where I would choose a ripe, juicy plum to accompany me on my brisk walk through the Boston Common. I now associate plums with bright, summer skies and the start of a brand new day. I like all kinds of plums, both sweet and tart, and any kind can be used in this catsup. Serve it with extremely spicy dishes, grilled or roasted chicken, pork, and fried plantains or sweet potatoes.

1 cup diced rhubarb
3 plums, diced

¼ **cup raisins**
½ **medium-size red onion, minced**
¾ **cup red wine vinegar**
¼ **cup brown sugar**
¼ **teaspoon salt**
¼ **teaspoon black pepper**

Combine all of the ingredients in a saucepan and simmer for 15 to 20 minutes over low heat, stirring occasionally. Remove the catsup from the heat. Process for 15 to 20 seconds in a food processor fitted with a steel blade.

Serve immediately or refrigerate. If refrigerated, the catsup should keep for 1 to 2 weeks.

YIELD: 1½ CUPS

Cherry Tomato-Date Catsup

❖❖❖

Homemade catsups can transform a hum-drum dish into a remarkable meal without a lot of effort. Dried fruits, like dates, figs, and apricots provide a slightly sweet dimension and balance the acidity of tomatoes and vinegar. The addition of a little fresh horseradish will leave a refreshing aftertaste.

½ pint cherry tomatoes, halved
4 ounces pitted dates, chopped
½ medium-size red onion, diced
2 to 3 garlic cloves, minced
1½ tablespoons peeled and minced fresh
   horseradish root
¾ cup red wine vinegar
¼ cup brown sugar

Combine all of the ingredients in a saucepan and bring to a simmer over medium heat. Simmer for 20 minutes, stirring occasionally. Remove from the heat and puree the mixture in a food processor fitted with a steel blade or in a blender for 30 seconds. The catsup will still be chunky.

Serve the catsup immediately or wrap and chill. If refrigerated, the catsup should keep for 7 to 10 days.

YIELD: 1½ CUPS

Apricot-Peach Catsup

❖❖

When I served Apricot-Peach Catsup at my restaurant, one customer asked me if I got ideas for my food creations in my sleep. I was just discovering what Europeans have known for years: Fruit and vegetables other than tomatoes produce a variety of delicious catsups. Serve this catsup with chicken, turkey, pork, and ham.

3 peaches, diced (do not peel)
½ medium-size onion, diced
½ cup dried apricots
1 cup apple cider vinegar
¼ cup brown sugar
¼ teaspoon salt
¼ teaspoon white pepper

Combine all of the ingredients in a saucepan and simmer for 10 minutes over medium heat, stirring occasionally. Allow the fruit mixture to cool for 10 minutes, and then puree it for 30 seconds in a food processor fitted with a steel blade or in a blender. The catsup will still be somewhat chunky.

Refrigerate the catsup until you are ready to use it. If refrigerated, the catsup should keep for 7 to 10 days.

YIELD: 2 CUPS

Cranberry Catsup

This sweet and tart catsup makes a colorful accompaniment to hamburgers, steaks, grilled chicken, and roast turkey. This batch is ideal for canning.

4 tomatoes, diced
12 ounces cranberries, fresh or frozen
1 medium-size onion, diced
1½ cups red wine vinegar
1 cup brown sugar
½ cup raisins
2 teaspoons onion powder
1 teaspoon grated orange zest
½ teaspoon black pepper
½ teaspoon salt
Juice of 1 orange

Combine all of the ingredients in a saucepan. Cook over low heat for 45 minutes, stirring occasionally. Remove the catsup from the heat and set aside for 10 minutes. When the catsup is slightly cooled, blend it in a food processor fitted with a steel blade or in a blender for 10 to 15 seconds. The catsup will still be slightly chunky.

Serve immediately or refrigerate. If refrigerated, the catsup should keep for about 2 weeks. To can, place the catsup in hot, sterilized, half-pint jars, seal, and process in boiling water bath for 20 minutes (see page 172).

YIELD: 6 CUPS

Mango Chutney

✧✧✧

Mangoes can be intimidating. How do you get at the fruit? At first I peeled it like a grapefruit but the sinewy, yellow-orange flesh clung tenaciously to its skin. I peeled another like a potato, using a paring knife, and that seemed the best way to extricate the flesh. Beneath the thin layer of flesh was a large, central pit shaped like a chicken's breastbone. Scraping the pit yielded more stringy pulp. The delicate flavor of this fruit, however, is a reward that makes extricating the flesh well worth the effort.

This homemade chutney is a little less sweet and has a stronger mango flavor than most commercial brands. For a fruity nuance, add ½ cup of chopped dried apricots, figs, dates, golden raisins or cherries to the condiment.

2 large, ripe mangoes, peeled, pitted, and chopped
¾ cup diced onion
1 apple or pear, diced (do not peel)
½ cup brown sugar
1 cup red wine vinegar
1 fresh red chili pepper, seeded and minced
1½ tablespoons minced fresh ginger root
4 to 6 garlic cloves, minced
¼ teaspoon salt
⅛ teaspoon cayenne pepper
⅛ teaspoon ground cloves

Combine all of the ingredients in a large saucepan and cook over low heat, stirring occasionally. Simmer for 35 to 40 minutes,

❖❖

until the mixture has a jam-like consistency.

Allow the chutney to cool to room temperature, and then refrigerate. Or can while still hot. To do so, pour the chutney into hot, sterilized, half-pint jars, seal, and process in boiling water bath for 20 minutes (see page 172).

YIELD: ABOUT 3 CUPS

Cranberry Chutney

❖❖

Cranberry chutney is such a staple at my restaurant that I buy 50 pounds of cranberries in the fall and freeze them for a year-round supply. Cranberries are one of the few fruits or vegetables that fully maintains its fresh flavor after it has been frozen.

12 ounces fresh or frozen cranberries
1 large apple, diced (do not peel)
1 pear, diced (do not peel)
1 medium-size onion, diced
8 to 10 garlic cloves, minced
2 tablespoons minced fresh ginger root
¾ cup brown sugar
½ cup raisins
2¼ cups red wine vinegar
½ teaspoon salt (optional)

Combine all of the ingredients in a large saucepan and cook over low heat, stirring occasionally. Simmer for 20 to 30 minutes, until the mixture has a jam-like consistency.

Allow the chutney to cool to room temperature, and then refrigerate. If refrigerated, the chutney should keep for 3 to 4 weeks. Or can while still hot. To do so, pour the chutney into hot, sterilized, half-pint jars, seal, and process in boiling water bath for 20 minutes (see page 172).

YIELD: 3½ CUPS

Pear-Walnut Chutney

✧✧

This is a chunky, nutty chutney laced with ginger. The riper the pears, the sweeter the chutney. Serve it with roast chicken, game hens, pork, or lamb.

3 pears, diced (do not peel)
1 onion, diced
1 cup coarsely chopped walnuts
2 tablespoons minced fresh ginger root
1¼ cups red wine vinegar or apple cider vinegar
¼ cup brown sugar
¼ teaspoon black pepper
¼ teaspoon salt

Combine all of the ingredients in a large saucepan and cook over low heat, stirring occasionally. Simmer for 35 to 40 minutes, until the mixture has a chunky, jam-like consistency.

Allow the chutney to cool to room temperature; then refrigerate. Or can while still hot. To do so, pour the chutney into hot, sterilized, half-pint jars, seal, and process in a boiling water bath for 20 minutes (see page 172).

YIELD: 3 CUPS

Fiery Tomato & Apple Chutney

❖❖❖

When I am in the mood for an incendiary chutney from hell, I turn to this one. This is not like eating a bowl of chili peppers; rather, it's that tomatoes are a perfect medium for extra spicy dishes. For an even hotter version, include the seeds of the jalapeño peppers and add a few teaspoons of chili-garlic paste (available where Oriental foods are sold).

3 to 4 ripe tomatoes, diced
2 apples, diced (do not peel)
½ medium-size onion, diced
1 cup red wine vinegar
1½ tablespoons minced fresh ginger
   root
3 to 4 garlic cloves, minced

½ cup raisins
3 to 4 jalapeño peppers, seeded and
   minced
¼ cup plus 2 tablespoons brown sugar
½ tablespoon ground cumin
½ teaspoon red hot sauce
¼ teaspoon black pepper
¼ teaspoon white pepper
⅛ teaspoon cayenne pepper
¼ teaspoon salt

Combine all of the ingredients in a large saucepan and cook over low heat, stirring occasionally. Simmer for 40 to 45 minutes, until the mixture has a chunky, jam-like consistency.

✤✤

Allow the chutney to cool to room temperature; then refrigerate. If refrigerated, the chutney should keep for 3 to 4 weeks. Or can while still hot. To do so, pour the chutney into hot, sterilized, half-pint jars, seal, and process in a boiling water bath for 20 minutes (see page 172).

YIELD: 3 CUPS

Apple-Nectarine Chutney

✧✧

The refreshing flavors of apples and nectarines penetrate this chutney. It is an irresistible way to use excess produce during harvest time, preserving the essence of the seasonal fruit. Peaches can be substituted for nectarines for an equally satisfying condiment. This recipe makes a large batch, ideal for canning.

10 ripe nectarines, diced (do not peel)
7 apples, diced (do not peel)
3 ripe pears, diced (do not peel)
2 medium-size onions, diced
7 cups red wine vinegar
1½ cups brown sugar
2 cups raisins
3 tablespoons minced fresh ginger root

10 to 12 garlic cloves, minced
1 tablespoon curry powder
1 tablespoon ground cumin
1 teaspoon white pepper
1 teaspoon red pepper flakes
½ teaspoon black pepper

Combine all of the ingredients in a large saucepan and cook over low heat, stirring occasionally. Simmer for 45 to 50 minutes, until the mixture has a jam-like consistency.

Allow the chutney to cool to room temperature; then refrigerate. Or can while still hot. To do so, pour the hot chutney into hot, sterilized, half-pint jars, seal, and process in a boiling water bath for 20 minutes (see page 172).

YIELD: ABOUT 3½ QUARTS

Rhubarb Chutney

✧✧

Rhubarb is crunchy and tart when eaten raw but forms a smooth vegetable puree when it is cooked. Its sourness is tempered by the sweetness of the apple, onion, and brown sugar, with the result being a mildly tart, mauve-colored condiment. Serve it with grilled chicken, pork, fish, or as a topping to a baked potato or winter squash.

1¼ pounds rhubarb, diced
1 medium-size onion, diced
1 apple, diced (do not peel)
1½ cups red wine vinegar
3 to 4 garlic cloves, minced
1 tablespoon minced fresh ginger root
½ cup brown sugar
½ teaspoon white pepper
¼ teaspoon salt

Combine all of the ingredients in a large saucepan and simmer over low heat, stirring occasionally, for 25 to 30 minutes, until the mixture has a jam-like consistency.

Allow the chutney to cool to room temperature; then refrigerate. Or can while still hot. To do so, pour the chutney into hot, sterilized, half-pint jars, seal, and process in boiling water bath for 20 minutes (see page 172).

YIELD: ABOUT 3 CUPS

83

Pineapple Chutney

❖❖

Pineapple is a natural ingredient for chutney, as its crunchy texture and citrusy aftertaste blend well with the tart and spicy components of chutneys. The result is very similar to a sweet-and-sour sauce and has very similar applications.

½ fresh pineapple, peeled, cored, and
   diced
1 pear, diced (do not peel)
1 apple, diced (do not peel)
1 medium-size onion, diced
1¾ cups apple cider vinegar
½ cup brown sugar
1 tablespoon minced fresh ginger root
4 to 5 garlic cloves, minced
1 tablespoon curry powder (optional)

2 teaspoons ground cumin (optional)
¼ teaspoon ground cloves
¼ teaspoon black pepper
¼ teaspoon white pepper
¼ teaspoon salt
3 to 4 drops red hot sauce
½ tablespoon minced fresh cilantro

Combine all of the ingredients, except the cilantro, in a large saucepan and cook over medium heat, stirring occasionally. Simmer for 45 minutes; then add the cilantro. Continue to cook for 5 to 10 minutes, reducing the heat as the mixture begins to thicken.

Allow the chutney to cool to room temperature; then refrigerate. If refrigerated, the chutney should keep for about 2 weeks.

❖❖

Or can while still hot. To do so, pour the hot chutney into hot, sterilized, half-pint jars, seal, and process in a boiling water bath for 20 minutes (see page 172).

YIELD: 4 CUPS

Dried Cherry & Peach Chutney

❖❖

Reconstituting dried cherries with peaches yields an intensely fruity condiment. Dried cherries may be hard to find, but they're well worth the search. Natural foods stores and specialty food shops may be the best places to look. This chutney is sweetened with maple syrup and honey, further heightening the natural flavors of the fruit.

3 peaches, diced (do not peel)
1 cup dried cherries
½ medium-size onion, diced
¼ cup pure maple syrup
⅛ cup honey
1 cup red wine vinegar
⅛ teaspoon salt
⅛ teaspoon white pepper
¼ cup fresh mint leaves or fresh basil

Combine all of the ingredients, except the mint, in a large saucepan and cook over low heat, stirring occasionally. Simmer for 15 minutes; then add the mint. Continue cooking for 5 to 10 minutes more, or until the mixture has a chunky, jam-like consistency.

Allow the chutney to cool to room temperature; then refrigerate. Or can while still hot. To do so, pour the chutney into hot, sterilized, half-pint jars, seal, and process in a boiling water bath for 20 minutes (see page 172).

YIELD: 2½ CUPS

Southwestern Corn Relish

❖❖

Quick and easy to prepare, this is a crunchy, sweet-and-sour relish with a hint of cilantro. Serve with roast turkey, chicken, or grilled or poached fish.

2 cups cooked corn kernels
2 cups diced, peeled jicama
½ cup diced red bell pepper
½ cup diced green pepper
1 jalapeño pepper, seeded and minced
1 cup distilled white vinegar
¼ cup brown sugar
2 tablespoons chopped fresh cilantro
    leaves
2 teaspoons mustard seeds
2 teaspoons ground cumin
¼ teaspoon white pepper
¼ teaspoon salt

Combine all of the ingredients in a mixing bowl and toss together thoroughly. Chill for at least 2 hours. Drain off any excess liquid before serving. If refrigerated, the relish should keep for 5 to 7 days.

YIELD: 5 CUPS

Cranberry-Fruit Relish

I always thought the canned cranberry relish that showed up every Thanksgiving was too sweet and more like Jell-O than relish. This relish, on the other hand, is partially sweetened with maple syrup and honey, and dried apricots add color and a fruity essence.

12 ounces cranberries, fresh or frozen and thawed
2 pears, diced (do not peel)
1 apple, diced (do not peel)
1 medium-size onion, diced
1 cup dried apricots, diced
½ cup raisins
2 cups red wine vinegar
½ cup pure maple syrup
¼ cup honey
1 tablespoon grated orange zest
½ teaspoon salt
¼ teaspoon black pepper
¼ teaspoon white pepper

Combine all of the ingredients and cook over low heat, stirring occasionally. Simmer for 30 to 35 minutes, or until the mixture reaches a chunky, jam-like consistency.

Cool to room temperature; then refrigerate for up to 2 weeks. Or can while still hot. To do so, spoon into hot, sterilized, half-pint jars, seal, and process in a boiling water bath for 20 minutes (see page 172).

YIELD: 6 CUPS

Beet-Cucumber Relish

Viva les beets! If you love beets, this relish is for you. If you don't love beets, this relish may convert you. Vividly purple, with a hint of cucumber, this relish is ideal for holiday meals that need a colorful accompaniment. Scrub the beets thoroughly before cooking or peel them with a vegetable peeler.

4 fresh, large, uncooked beets, diced
2 cucumbers, peeled and sliced
10 scallions, diced
2½ cups red wine vinegar
½ cup brown sugar
3 tablespoons minced fresh dill weed
½ teaspoon black pepper
½ teaspoon salt

Combine all of the ingredients in a saucepan over low heat. Stirring occasionally, cook for 45 minutes, or until the beets are easily pierced with a fork.

Let the mixture cool to room temperature; then refrigerate. If refrigerated, the relish should keep for 7 to 10 days. Or can while still hot. To do so, spoon the relish into hot, sterilized, half-pint jars, seal, and process in a boiling water bath for 20 minutes (see page 172).

YIELD: 3 CUPS

Tangerine-Fig Relish

✤✤

A dried fig is a wrinkled, pear-shaped fruit with a sweet, chewy interior. Like other dried fruits, figs are natural ingredients for relishes because they retain their form and natural sweetness after cooking for a long period of time with vinegar. The result is a chunky, sweet-and-tart relish. Tangerines contribute a pleasant, tangy nuance. Serve with roast pork, turkey, or chicken, or over steamed vegetables.

1 pound dried figs, chopped
1 medium-size red onion, diced
Juice of 5 tangerines
¾ cup apple cider vinegar
¼ cup brown sugar
1 tablespoon grated tangerine zest

Combine all of the ingredients in a saucepan and bring to a simmer over medium heat. Simmer for 20 minutes, stirring occasionally. Allow the relish to cool to room temperature; then chill for at least 2 hours before serving. If refrigerated, the relish should keep for 7 to 10 days.

YIELD: 4 CUPS

Pecan-Banana Relish

The smoothness of balsamic vinegar, which is aged longer than other vinegars and is less acidic, unites the natural sweetness of banana with the nuttiness of pecans. This relish is good with roast lamb, pork, turkey, chicken, or Cornish game hens. For a delightful spin, add ½ cup of chopped dried apricots, dates, figs, or raisins.

¼ cup balsamic vinegar
1 teaspoon Dijon-style mustard
¼ teaspoon white pepper
⅛ teaspoon salt
½ cup olive oil
2 bananas, peeled and diced
1 cup chopped pecans

In a mixing bowl, whisk together the vinegar, mustard, white pepper and salt. Gradually whisk the oil into the mixture. Add the bananas and pecans and toss thoroughly. Chill for at least 1 hour before serving. If refrigerated, the relish should keep for 3 days.

YIELD: 2 CUPS

Mulligatawny

Mulligatawny, also referred to as curried chicken and apple soup, is an Indian broth brimming with wonderful, complex flavors. This is a favorite soup of an old girlfriend of mine. Instead of sending chocolates or roses, I would make mulligatawny for her. I would make it slightly different every time by adding a different chutney, dried fruit, or seasoning to the broth.

2½ tablespoons butter
1 onion, diced
1 green pepper, seeded and diced
1 carrot, diced
½ cup diced celery
6 garlic cloves, minced
1 tablespoon minced fresh ginger root
1 tablespoon minced fresh parsley

1 apple, cored and diced (do not peel)
6 cups hot chicken or turkey stock
1 pound cooked chicken or turkey, diced
½ cup canned crushed tomatoes
½ cup Cranberry Chutney (page 78), Apple-Nectarine Chutney (page 82), Mango Chutney (page 76), or Pineapple Chutney (page 84)
½ cup raisins or chopped dried apricots
1½ tablespoons curry powder
2 teaspoons ground cumin
1 teaspoon salt
½ teaspoon turmeric
¼ teaspoon ground cloves
¼ teaspoon black pepper
⅛ teaspoon cayenne pepper
⅛ teaspoon white pepper

❖❖❖

In large saucepan, melt the butter and add
the onion, green pepper, carrot, celery,
garlic, ginger root, and parsley. Cook over
medium heat until the vegetables are soft,
stirring occasionally. Add the apple,
chicken stock, chicken, crushed tomatoes,
chutney, dried fruit, and seasonings. Bring
the mixture to a simmer and continue cooking over low heat for 15 minutes, stirring
occasionally. Pour into soup bowls and
serve immediately.

YIELD: 4 TO 6 SERVINGS

Curried Sweet Potato Salad

✦✦✦

As a child I refused to eat yams. I had trouble with the way they looked coming out of a can, and the name itself was disturbing. Years later, I began using fresh sweet potatoes in my recipes, and it was with a certain irony that I realized that the dreaded canned yam was really an adulterated sweet potato. This tuber was meant to be prepared fresh from the land, not from the can.

4 large, unpeeled sweet potatoes,
   scrubbed and coarsely chopped
10 to 12 broccoli florets
1½ cups minced celery
½ red onion, thinly sliced
½ cup dried currants or raisins
½ cup mayonnaise (see page 33)
½ cup sour cream

½ cup Apple-Nectarine Chutney (page
   82), Rhubarb Chutney (page 83), or
   Cranberry Chutney (page 78)
1½ tablespoons curry powder
2 teaspoons minced fresh parsley
1 teaspoon turmeric
1 teaspoon ground cumin
½ teaspoon salt
⅛ teaspoon black pepper
⅛ teaspoon cayenne pepper
½ teaspoon red hot sauce

Place the potatoes in boiling water to cover and boil for about 15 minutes, or until the potatoes are easily pierced by a fork, but not mushy. Drain and chill under cold running water.

Blanch the broccoli in boiling water to cover for 3 to 4 minutes. Drain and chill under cold running water.

Combine all of the ingredients in a mixing bowl and toss together thoroughly. Chill for at least 1 hour before serving.

YIELD: 6 TO 8 SERVINGS

Warm Spring Salad

✧✧✧

I must confess, before I started this cookbook, I didn't think too much of beets. It was another bias rooted in my youth; seeing them canned didn't appeal to me. They were frequently served at the school cafeteria, but I don't think anyone ever ate them. But when I cooked my first bunch of fresh beets, my attitude quickly changed. What a difference! When you combine fresh beets with a few other crunchy, colorful vegetables, such as asparagus and carrots, you have a magnificent salad. To complete the picture, spoon a little relish or chutney over the top. It tastes as good as it looks.

1 large fresh beet, peeled and cut into 2-inch matchsticks
12 asparagus stalks, halved

1 large carrot, cut into 2-inch matchsticks
1½ tablespoons olive or other vegetable oil or Dijon-Style Mustard Vinaigrette (page 165)
4 to 5 leaves leaf or romaine lettuce
1½ cups Cranberry-Fruit Relish (page 88), Tangerine-Fig Relish (page 90), Pineapple Chutney (page 84), Mango Chutney (page 76), or Dried Cherry & Peach Chutney (page 86)
2 tablespoons hulled sesame seeds

Cook the beet in boiling water to cover for 6 to 8 minutes, or until soft. Drain and discard the water.

Place the asparagus in boiling water to cover and boil for 3 minutes. Drain and discard the water.

Toss together the beet, asparagus, carrot, and oil in a mixing bowl. Arrange the vegetables on a bed of leaf lettuce. Spoon the relish or chutney over the vegetables and sprinkle 1 to 2 teaspoons of the sesame seeds over the salad. Serve as a first course or as a side dish to fish or pasta.

YIELD: 4 TO 6 SERVINGS

Arugula & Feta Salad

✦✦

Arugula is a zippy, leafy herb that adds spice to a salad of fresh greens. The beet relish contributes a nice splash of color and flavor.

½ cup Beet-Cucumber Relish (page 89)
¼ cup olive or other vegetable oil
1 small head leaf lettuce, torn
1½ cups chopped arugula
¾ cup shredded jicama
¾ cup shredded carrot
½ red onion, thinly sliced
1 tomato, cut into 8 wedges
½ cup feta or crumbled blue cheese

Place the relish in a food processor fitted with a steel blade and process for 15 seconds. While the machine is still running, drizzle the oil into the relish and process for another 10 seconds. Set aside.

Place the leaf lettuce on the centers of 4 round plates. Spread the arugula over the lettuce. Place the jicama, carrot, red onion, and tomato around the perimeter of each of the plates. Spoon the relish mixture over each salad. Top with the crumbled cheese and serve at once.

YIELD: 4 SERVINGS

Hazelnut Tuna

❖❖❖

This is an easy and elegant way to dress up a fish. Swordfish and mahimahi steaks can also be used.

½ cup Rhubarb Chutney (page 83), warmed
2 tablespoons light cream
2 cups finely chopped hazelnuts
2 teaspoons crushed black peppercorns
1½ pounds fresh tuna steaks
2 tablespoons butter
2 tablespoons olive oil
1 lemon, quartered

Preheat the oven to 400° F.

Mix the chutney and cream together and set aside.

Combine the hazelnuts and peppercorns on a plate. Press both sides of the tuna firmly into the mixture.

In an ovenproof skillet, melt the butter with the oil. Add the steaks to the pan and cook for 3 minutes over moderately high heat. Gently flip the steaks and continue cooking for 3 minutes. Finish cooking the tuna in the oven for 5 to 7 minutes or until the center is light burgundy.

Remove the steaks to warm plates and spoon the chutney cream sauce over them. Squeeze lemon over the fish and serve immediately.

YIELD: 4 SERVINGS

Curried Shrimp & Pasta Salad

Ithaca's countryside is resplendent with brilliant foliage in autumn. I like to hike along one of the area's scenic gorges or parks, or take an afternoon drive along the lake. This salad's warm flavors and colors match the mood of a breezy autumn day—its an ideal meal to take on a picnic in the fall.

8 ounces dry pasta spirals
6 broccoli florets
20 to 24 medium-size shrimp, peeled, deveined, and cooked
2 apples, diced (do not peel)
½ cup raisins
½ pint cherry tomatoes, halved
½ red onion, minced
1¼ cups fresh shredded coconut

½ cup Cranberry Chutney (page 78), Pineapple Chutney (page 84), Fiery Tomato & Apple Chutney (page 80), Mango Chutney (page 76), or Apple-Nectarine Chutney (page 82)
½ cup sour cream
½ cup mayonnaise (see page 33) or plain yogurt
1½ tablespoons curry powder
½ tablespoon ground cumin
½ teaspoon red hot sauce
¼ teaspoon salt
¼ teaspoon turmeric
¼ teaspoon ground cloves
⅛ teaspoon cayenne pepper

✧✧

Bring a large pot of water to a boil, add the pasta, and boil until al dente, about 8 to 10 minutes, stirring occasionally. Drain and cool under cold running water.

Blanch the broccoli in boiling water to cover for 3 to 4 minutes. Drain and cool under cold running water.

In a large mixing bowl, combine the pasta and broccoli with the remaining ingredients and mix thoroughly. Wrap tightly and chill for at least 2 hours before serving.

YIELD: 4 TO 6 SERVINGS

Grilled Trout with Corn Relish

❖❖❖

Every April the streams in upstate New York are filled with trout fishing enthusiasts of all ages and backgrounds. They rise before the sun comes up, wade into the streams or camp on the banks, and search for moving shadows in the water. It is gratifying to know that in our high-tech, couch-potato society there still exists a breed of individuals who brave nature's elements in pursuit of sport and adventure. Southwestern Corn Relish makes a nice accompaniment to freshly caught or store-bought trout.

**4 (8-ounce) rainbow trout, dressed
    and deboned**
⅛ cup olive or other vegetable oil
1 tablespoon paprika

**2 tablespoons butter (for panfried
    version only)**
1 lemon, quartered
**1½ cups Southwestern Corn Relish
    (page 87)**

Preheat the grill until the coals are gray to white.

Open the trout and lightly baste the flesh with the oil. Lightly oil the grill and lay the trout flesh side down over the heat.

After 1 minute, loosen the trout from the grill with a spatula to prevent sticking. Flip the trout after 3 or 4 minutes and cook skin side down just long enough to crisp the skin, about 2 minutes. Sprinkle paprika lightly over the trout while the flesh side is up. Flip the flesh side back onto the grill and finish

✣✣

cooking until the trout flesh is clear white in the center.

To panfry the fish, melt 2 tablespoons butter over moderately high heat in a sauté pan. Lay the trout, flesh side down, in the pan. Flip after 4 to 5 minutes, reduce the heat, and sprinkle paprika over the flesh. Flip again and continue cooking until the flesh is white in the center.

Remove the trout to a warm plate. Squeeze lemon over each fish and serve immediately. Pass the relish at the table.

YIELD: 4 SERVINGS

Coconut-Marinated Swordfish

Swordfish has a mild flavor with a firm, steak-like texture. It is ideal for grilling, broiling, or baking. A light marinade is an easy way to flavor swordfish. Try this coconut marinade or the marinade for Grapefruit-Grilled Mahimahi (page 106). It is served with a colorful, tangy relish for extra flavor.

2 cups unsweetened coconut milk
(available where Oriental food is
sold, or see page 151)
¼ cup lime juice
¼ cup dry sherry
½ cup chopped fresh mint or cilantro
leaves
1 teaspoon cayenne pepper or
Blackened Seasonings (page 167)

¼ teaspoon salt
1 teaspoon paprika
4 (8-ounce) swordfish steaks
Lemon wedges
1½ cups Southwestern Corn Relish
(page 87), Beet-Cucumber Relish
(page 89), or Cranberry-Fruit Relish
(page 88)

Combine the coconut milk, lime juice, sherry, mint, cayenne, and salt in a shallow glass baking dish. Add the swordfish and chill for 3 hours. Turn swordfish over after 1½ hours.

Preheat the oven to 425° F.

Place the swordfish on a greased baking pan and sprinkle paprika over the fish. Bake

✧✧✧

for 12 to 15 minutes, or until the fish is opaque in the center.

If you are grilling the fish, preheat the grill until the coals are gray to white. Remove the swordfish from the marinade and pat dry. Lightly oil the grill and place the swordfish over the heat. Lightly sprinkle paprika over the fish. Turn after 5 to 7 minutes. Continue grilling for 5 to 7 minutes more, or until the swordfish is opaque in the center.

Remove the fish to warm plates. Squeeze lemon over each fish and pass the relish at the table.

YIELD: 4 SERVINGS

Grapefruit-Grilled Mahimahi

❖❖

My sister gave me the idea for using a grapefruit marinade. Well, sort of. She mentioned that she had recently tried a delicious grapefruit vinaigrette. I thought that if grapefruit juice could make a good vinaigrette, it might make a tasty marinade. I tried it with mahimahi, a delicately flavored fish, and it worked. The grapefruit marinade heightened the flavor of the fish without overpowering it. Serve the fish with a colorful, strongly flavored relish or chutney. Fresh swordfish, tuna, or red snapper can also be used.

Juice of 4 grapefruits (about 2 cups)
½ cup dry sherry
2 tablespoons sesame oil

¼ teaspoon cayenne pepper
¼ teaspoon salt
1½ pounds mahimahi steaks
1 tablespoon paprika
2 cups Beet-Cucumber Relish (page 89),
  Cranberry-Fruit Relish (page 88),
  Rhubarb Chutney (page 83), or
  Mango Chutney (page 76)

Combine the grapefruit juice, sherry, sesame oil, cayenne, and salt in a shallow baking dish. Add the mahimahi steaks and refrigerate for 4 hours. Turn over the steaks after 2 hours.

Preheat the grill until the coals are gray to white.

Remove the mahimahi from the mari-

❖❖

nade. Lightly oil the grill and place the fish over the heat. Lightly sprinkle paprika over the fish. Turn after 5 to 7 minutes. Continue grilling for 5 to 7 minutes more, or until the fish is opaque in the center.

Remove the fish to warm plates and pass the relish or chutney at the table.

YIELD: 4 SERVINGS

Herbed Chicken Sandwich

✦✦✦

Vinaigrette dressing is not confined to a tossed salad in my restaurant. It is one of my favorite marinades for chicken. It imparts a tart, herbal flavor that blends well with a variety of condiments.

Vinaigrette Marinade

1 cup red wine vinegar
2 cups vegetable oil
2 tablespoons Dijon-style mustard
1 tablespoon honey
2 teaspoons dried tarragon
2 teaspoons dried rosemary
2 teaspoons dried thyme leaves
1 teaspoon dried oregano
1 teaspoon dried basil
1 teaspoon dried chives

1 teaspoon black pepper
½ teaspoon salt

Sandwich

2 (8-ounce) boneless and skinless
   chicken breasts, pounded and halved
4 warm rolls
½ cup Apricot-Peach Catsup
   (page 74), Cherry Tomato-Date
   Catsup (page 73), Pesto Mayonnaise
   (page 39), or Greek Yogurt Sauce
   (page 141)
4 to 5 leaves leaf or romaine lettuce,
   torn
1 tomato, sliced
½ red onion, thinly sliced

Whisk together all of the ingredients to make the vinaigrette marinade.

Add the chicken breasts and marinate in the refrigerator for at least 3 hours before grilling. Stir the marinade after 1 hour.

Before you are ready to grill, preheat the grill until the coals are gray to white.

Remove the chicken from the marinade, shaking off any excess marinade, and place it on the hot grill. Cook for 4 to 5 minutes and then flip. Continue cooking for about 4 minutes more, or until the chicken is white in the center.

To broil the chicken instead, place the chicken on a broiling pan and broil 6 inches from the heat source for 7 to 10 minutes; then turn the chicken over. Continue broil-ing for 4 to 6 minutes more, or until the chicken is white in the center.

Place the chicken on the rolls, spoon the condiment over it, and top with lettuce, tomato, and red onion. Serve immediately.

YIELD: 4 SERVINGS

Variation:
Vinaigrette-Grilled Chicken. This recipe can be adapted to make a dinner-size serv-ing. Marinate a full 6-ounce chicken breast for each serving, grill according to the above directions, serve over rice, and top the chicken with one of the condiments.

Chicken Teriyaki Sandwich

✧✧

This is the most popular sandwich at my restaurant. For the best marinade, use a soy sauce that has no added MSG or sugar, and don't marinate longer than the recommended 4 hours. Almost any condiment in this book can be served over the chicken; I've recommended a few of my favorites.

Teriyaki Marinade

1 cup soy sauce
1 cup Worcestershire sauce
1 cup vegetable oil
½ cup orange juice
2 tablespoons minced fresh ginger root
8 to 10 garlic cloves, minced
1 tablespoon sugar
1 teaspoon black pepper
6 drops red hot sauce

Sandwich

2 (8-ounce to 9-ounce) chicken breasts, skinless, boneless, pounded, and halved
4 sandwich rolls, warmed
1 cup Rhubarb Chutney (page 83), Apple-Nectarine Chutney (page 82), Cranberry Chutney (page 78), Cranberry Catsup (page 75), Sun-Dried Tomato Catsup (page 71), Pesto Mayonnaise (page 39), Apple-Pear Mustard (page 43), or Red Tomato Salsa (page 3)
4 to 5 leaves leaf or romaine lettuce, torn
1 tomato, sliced

✦✦

Combine all of the marinade ingredients, whisk well, and chill for 1 hour.

Place the chicken breasts in the marinade and marinate in the refrigerator for 4 hours. After 2 hours, stir the marinade. Preheat the grill until the coals are gray to white.

Remove the chicken breasts from the marinade and drain or shake off the excess marinade. Oil the grill and place the chicken breasts on the grill. Cook as you would a medium-rare burger, about 4 to 5 minutes on each side, until the flesh is off-white in the center.

Serve the chicken teriyaki on warmed sandwich rolls and spoon the condiment over each sandwich. Garnish with lettuce and tomato. Serve with Roasted Garlic Potatoes (page 128), Curried Sweet Potato Salad (page 94), cole slaw, or a tossed salad.

YIELD: 4 SERVINGS

Variation:
Grilled Chicken Teriyaki. This recipe can be adapted to make a dinner-size serving. Marinate a full 6-ounce chicken breast for each serving, grill according to the above directions, serve over rice, and top the chicken with one of the condiments.

Tandoori-Roasted Chicken

The tandoori marinade is an excellent way to flavor and tenderize chicken drumsticks and thighs. This is an especially spicy marinade. For an exotic meal, serve the chicken with an array of colorful relishes and chutneys and Vegetables with Fiery Chutney (page 122).

Tandoori Marinade

3 cups plain yogurt
½ cup red wine vinegar
¼ cup olive oil
2 tablespoons minced fresh ginger root
8 to 10 garlic cloves, minced
2 tablespoons ground cumin
1 tablespoon ground coriander
1 tablespoon paprika
1 tablespoon garam masala
   (available where Indian food is sold)
1 teaspoon ground cloves
2 teaspoons red hot sauce
1 teaspoon salt
½ teaspoon cayenne pepper
½ teaspoon black pepper

Chicken

4 chicken thighs, fat removed
4 chicken drumsticks, fat removed
1½ cups Mango Chutney (page 76),
   Cranberry Chutney (page 78),
   Sun-Dried Tomato Catsup
   (page 71), Beet-Cucumber Relish
   (page 89), or Cranberry-Fruit Relish
   (page 88)

✥✥

Combine all of the ingredients for the marinade in a mixing bowl and whisk thoroughly. Place the chicken pieces in a bowl
and cover with the tandoori marinade.
Refrigerate for 4 hours. Stir the marinade
after 2 hours.

Preheat the oven to 400° F.

Remove the chicken from the marinade
and place on a rack over a pan. Bake for 35
to 40 minutes, or until the meat is easily
separated from the bone.

Serve immediately with rice or Herbed
Couscous (page 168). Pass the chutney,
catsup, or relish at the table.

YIELD: 4 SERVINGS

Curried Chicken with Pineapple

❖❖❖

Curry powder is a blend of turmeric, coriander, cumin, cinnamon, ginger, fenugreek, dry mustard, peppercorns, pepper flakes, and cayenne. It is found in Indian and Thai cuisines and is often used to bridge the sweet elements of a dish with the tart. Store-bought curries vary in degree of spiciness, but they're easy to adjust by adding cayenne and turmeric for more heat, or cumin and cinnamon for less.

2 tablespoons butter
1½ pounds boneless, skinless chicken breasts, diced
1 large onion, diced
2 cups diced fresh pineapple
1 jalapeño pepper, seeded and minced

2 cups Cranberry Chutney (page 78), or Mango Chutney (page 76)
1 tablespoon curry powder
2 cups Mint Raita (page 142), Banana Raita (page 143), or plain yogurt

Melt the butter in a large sauté pan. Add the chicken and cook for 3 minutes over moderate heat. Add the onion, pineapple, and pepper and continue cooking, stirring occasionally. When the chicken is white in the center, reduce the heat, stir in the chutney and curry, and simmer for 1 minute. Serve immediately over warm rice, and spoon the raita over the curry.

YIELD: 3 TO 4 SERVINGS

Chicken Indienne

❖❖❖❖❖❖❖❖❖❖❖❖❖❖❖❖❖❖❖❖❖❖❖❖❖❖❖❖❖❖❖❖❖❖❖❖❖❖❖

This is the perfect dish to showcase the deep, penetrating flavors of chutney. Serve this dish with a soothing condiment like Mint Raita or Banana Raita.

2 tablespoons butter
1½ pounds skinless and boneless
   chicken breasts, diced
2 medium-size tomatoes, diced
1 large onion, diced
2 tablespoons dry white wine
1 tablespoon curry powder
2 teaspoons ground cumin
⅛ teaspoon black pepper
⅛ teaspoon cayenne pepper
2 cups Cranberry Chutney (page 78),
   Apple-Nectarine Chutney (page 82),
   or Pineapple Chutney (page 84)

2 cups Mint Raita (page 142), Banana
   Raita (page 143), or plain yogurt

Melt the butter in a sauté pan. Add the chicken, tomatoes, and onion and sauté over high heat. Add the wine after 2 to 3 minutes. Cook for 7 to 10 minutes, or until the chicken is white in the center. Add the curry powder, cumin, black pepper, cayenne pepper, and chutney; then reduce the heat. Bring the mixture to a simmer, stirring frequently. Continue to simmer for 1 more minute.

Serve over hot rice. Spoon some raita over the chicken and pass the extra raita at the table.

YIELD: 3 TO 4 SERVINGS

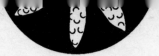

Couscous-Stuffed Game Hens

✦✦

Cornish game hens make an easy, elegant meal. Their meat is tender and moist and the couscous makes a light, flavorful stuffing.

1 cup uncooked couscous
½ cup diced red onion
¼ cup raisins or minced dried apricots
1 tablespoon dried rosemary leaves
2 teaspoons dried tarragon
1 teaspoon dried thyme leaves
½ teaspoon salt
½ teaspoon black pepper
½ cup warm water
½ cup blackberry brandy or other
  fruit-flavored brandy
½ cup water

4 (1½-pound) rock Cornish game hens,
  rinsed and patted dry
2 tablespoons olive oil
1½ cups Pecan-Banana Relish (page
  91), Pear-Walnut Chutney (page 79),
  or Dried Cherry & Peach Chutney
  (page 86)

Preheat the oven to 425° F.

Combine the couscous, onion, raisins, seasonings, and ½ cup warm water in a mixing bowl.

Combine the brandy with the remaining ½ cup water and set aside.

Fill the cavities of the hens with the couscous mixture and truss by inserting trussing pins on either side of the cavities and wrap-

✥✥

ping twine around the pins, partially enclosing the cavities. Trussing helps keep the stuffing in the bird. Rub each hen with the olive oil.

Place the hens breast side up on a rack set in a baking pan and bake for 20 minutes, basting every 10 minutes with the brandy mixture. Reduce the heat to 350° F. and bake for 35 minutes more, or until the meat is easily pulled from the bone.

Place the birds on warm plates and remove the truss strings. Serve immediately and pass the relish, or chutney at the table.

YIELD: 4 SERVINGS

Pork Loin with Apricots & Dates

❖❖

Pork, like chicken, is mildly flavored and benefits from the addition of strongly flavored condiments, such as chutney and mustard. It also blends well with fruit. Promoted as "the other white meat," pork is usually leaner and better trimmed than a few years ago and is making a comeback.

3 tablespoons butter
2 pounds boneless pork loin, diced
1 medium-size onion, diced
2 cups halved dried apricots
2 cups halved dried pitted dates
4 cups Apple-Nectarine Chutney
  (page 82), Cranberry Chutney (page
  78), or Mango Chutney (page 76)

Melt the butter in a large sauté pan. Add the pork and onion and cook over moderately high heat. After 3 minutes, add the apricots and dates. Stir occasionally and cook until the pork is white in the center and slightly browned on the outside. Add the chutney and bring the mixture to a simmer. Continue cooking for 1 more minute, stirring frequently. Serve immediately over warm rice.

YIELD: 4 TO 5 SERVINGS

Pecan-Breaded Pork Chops

✦✦✦

This is a quick and easy way to serve pork chops. Two friends of mine, Jessica and Emily, grew up on pork chops (their own admission) and pronounced this dish one of the best they've ever had.

2 eggs, beaten
¼ cup milk
1½ pounds center-cut loin pork chops
1½ cups pecans, minced
3 tablespoons butter
2 cups Beet-Cucumber Relish (page 89),
   Cranberry-Fruit Relish (page 88),
   Apricot-Peach Catsup (page 74), or
   Rhubarb-Plum Catsup (page 72)

Preheat the oven to 375° F.

Combine the eggs with the milk in a shallow mixing bowl. Soak the pork chops in the egg mixture. Place the pecans on a flat surface and dredge the pork chops in the pecans. Press the pecans into both sides of the pork chops.

Melt the butter in a large ovenproof skillet. Add the pork chops and cook over medium heat for 3 to 4 minutes. Turn the pork chops over and cook for 3 minutes more. Place the pork chops in the oven and bake for 5 to 7 minutes, or until the pork chops are off-white in the center.

Remove the chops to warm plates and serve immediately with rice. Pass the relish or catsup at the table.

YIELD: 4 SERVINGS

Roquefort-Stuffed Burger

✥✥

When I get a craving for a burger, I usually respond to it with an elaborate production. I start with quality ground beef, fill it with cheese or spices, and then top it with an assortment of ingredients: jalapeños, avocados, scallions, black beans, corn, and even crabmeat. I mound the toppings high and grab plenty of napkins.

1½ pounds ground chuck or beef
¾ pound roquefort cheese, crumbled
4 hamburger buns, warmed
1 cup catsup (pages 70 to 75)
1 ripe avocado, peeled and slivered
1 red onion, slivered
1 tomato, sliced
4 to 5 leaves leaf or romaine lettuce,
    torn

Preheat the grill until the coals are gray to white.

Divide the ground beef into 4 round patties. Spoon 2 tablespoons of cheese into the center of each patty and re-form into a burger, enveloping the cheese.

When the fire is ready, place the stuffed burgers onto the grill and cook to desired doneness (about 3 minutes on each side for rare, 6 minutes for medium, and 8 to 9 minutes for well done).

Serve on warm rolls and spoon the catsup over the burger. Top with avocado, red onion, tomato, and lettuce. Roasted Garlic Potatoes (page 128) makes a nice side dish.

YIELD: 4 SERVINGS

Stuffed Acorn Squash

Acorn squash has a rich, pumpkin-like flesh that combines well with sweet condiments. The shell is dark green with streaks of orange and makes an attractive bowl for the relish filling.

2 cups water
2 acorn squashes, halved and seeded
½ cup melted butter
4 cups Tangerine-Fig Relish (page 90), warmed
1 cup Banana Raita (page 143), Mint Raita (page 142), or plain yogurt

Preheat the oven to 400° F.

Pour the water into a baking pan and place the squash halves in the pan sitting up like a bowl. Baste the inner surface with butter and bake for 35 to 45 minutes, or until the squash is soft.

With an ice cream scoop, remove the squash pulp, leaving the shell intact. Place the pulp in a mixing bowl, add the remaining butter and the Tangerine-Fig Relish, and combine thoroughly. Spoon the relish-pulp mixture back into the acorn shell and top with raita. Serve immediately.

YIELD: 4 SERVINGS

Vegetables with Fiery Chutney

❖❖❖

Most vegetables should be lightly sautéed and served while still crunchy and colorful; too often they are overcooked or drowned in butter and have lost their identity. Every time I am faced with poorly prepared vegetables, I am reminded of an old New Yorker cartoon that depicts a husband and wife at dinner, the husband glaring at the vegetables on his plate. "It's broccoli, dear," the wife says. "I say it's spinach and I say the hell with it!" the husband replies. I try to think of ways that would entice people to enjoy their vegetables. Cooking them with chutney is one way to jazz up vegetables without a lot of effort or extra calories.

6 broccoli florets
6 cauliflower florets
2 tablespoons butter
1½ cups chopped eggplant (do not peel)
1 tomato, diced
4 mushrooms, sliced
1 small green pepper, seeded and diced
¼ cup peas, fresh or frozen and thawed
1¼ cups Fiery Tomato & Apple Chutney (page 80)
1 tablespoon curry powder
½ cup Banana Raita (page 143), Mint Raita (page 142), or plain yogurt

❖❖❖

Place the broccoli and cauliflower in boiling water to cover and boil for 3 minutes. Drain and chill under cold running water.

Melt the butter in a sauté pan and add the eggplant, broccoli, cauliflower, tomato, mushrooms, and green pepper. Sauté for 5 to 7 minutes over medium heat. Add the peas, chutney, and curry powder and bring the mixture to a simmer, stirring frequently. Cook for about 30 seconds longer. Serve as a side dish or over rice as a main course topped with the raita.

YIELD: 4 SIDE DISH OR 2 DINNER SERVINGS

Scallion-Pepper Corn Bread

✥✥

When I first heard it was a midwestern tradition to smother corn bread with catsup, I was skeptical but curious and decided to try it. I baked a corn bread filled with scallions and hot peppers, and while it was still warm, I spread Cherry Tomato-Date Catsup over it. The result erased any skepticism that I harbored. For a light, satisfying meal, serve the corn bread with Black Bean Soup (page 144) or Mulligatawny (page 92) and a tossed salad.

1 cup yellow cornmeal
1 cup all-purpose flour
¼ cup sugar
1 tablespoon baking powder
½ teaspoon salt

1 teaspoon coarsely crushed black
   peppercorns
2 eggs, beaten
½ cup buttermilk
½ cup milk
¼ cup melted butter
½ cup chopped scallions
2 to 3 jalapeño peppers, seeded and
   minced
1 cup Cherry Tomato-Date Catsup
   (page 73), Basic Tomato Catsup
   (page 70), or Apricot-Peach Catsup
   (page 74)

Preheat the oven to 375° F. Grease an 8-inch square baking pan.

   Combine the cornmeal, flour, sugar,

✠✠✠

baking powder, salt, and peppercorns in a bowl and mix together. In a separate bowl, whisk the eggs, buttermilk, milk, and butter together and add the scallions and peppers.

Fold the liquid ingredients into the dry. Gently fold until the mixture forms a batter. Pour the batter into the baking pan and bake for 20 to 25 minutes, or until the crust is lightly brown and a toothpick inserted in the center comes out clean.

Cool on a rack for about 10 minutes. Then cut into squares and spread a few tablespoons of catsup over the top. Serve at once.

YIELD: 4 TO 6 SERVINGS

Pumpkin Scones with Chutney

❖❖❖

Chutney makes a fancy spread for biscuits and scones. Serving chutney in place of jams or jellies is another way to introduce people to the joys of chutney.

2¼ cups all-purpose unbleached flour
2½ teaspoons baking powder
1 teaspoon cinnamon
½ teaspoon salt
¼ cup brown sugar
¼ cup plus 2 tablespoons butter, softened
1 cup canned or cooked pumpkin puree
⅔ cup milk
1 cup chopped pecans, walnuts, or cashews

1 cup Rhubarb Chutney (page 83), Dried Cherry & Peach Chutney (page 86), Mango Chutney (page 76), or Apricot-Peach Catsup (page 74)
4 ounces cream cheese (optional)

Preheat the oven to 425° F. Lightly grease 2 baking sheets.

Combine the flour, baking powder, cinnamon, salt, and brown sugar in a mixing bowl. Cut in the butter until the dough resembles coarse meal. Add the pumpkin and milk and fold until fully incorporated. Fold in the nuts.

With a spoon that holds about 2 tablespoons of batter, scoop the batter onto the baking sheets. Press the dough into round

✢✢

balls and leave 2 to 3 inches between each drop of dough. Scoop all of the batter onto the pans.

Bake for 12 to 15 minutes, or until the crusts of the scones are light brown.

Remove to wire racks and let cool to room temperature. Spread cream cheese and chutney over the scones and pass the extra chutney at the table. Serve with a hot beverage or milk.

YIELD: 15 TO 16 SCONES

Roasted Garlic Potatoes

✦✦✦

When I was 10 years old, I planted my first garden: carrots, lettuce, cucumbers, and potatoes. All of the vegetables, except the potatoes, were either eaten by rabbits, run over by the lawn mower, or simply shriveled up and died. When it was time to unearth the potatoes, however, my despondency turned into elation. I uncovered tuber after tuber buried beneath the plants. It was like finding a buried treasure.

8 garlic cloves, minced
½ cup olive oil or other vegetable oil
1½ tablespoons dried rosemary leaves
½ teaspoon salt
1 teaspoon dried red pepper flakes
1 teaspoon paprika
4 large red potatoes, quartered

1 cup Basic Tomato Catsup (page 70), Sun-Dried Tomato Catsup (page 71), Cherry Tomato-Date Catsup (page 73), or Fiery Tomato & Apple Chutney (page 80)

Preheat the oven to 375° F.

Combine the garlic, oil, rosemary, salt, and pepper flakes in a bowl and mix well.

Place potatoes on a greased baking pan and lightly baste them with the oil mixture. Lightly sprinkle the paprika over the potatoes. Bake for 35 minutes or until the potatoes are easily pierced by a fork. Toss with the remaining oil mixture and let stand for 5 minutes. Remove from oil, spoon catsup or chutney over potatoes, and serve at once.

YIELD: 4 SIDE DISH SERVINGS

4
International Condiments

✛✛

For much of my life, I have eaten apples from New York and Washington, oranges from Florida, onions from Georgia, cheese from Wisconsin, potatoes from Idaho, cranberries from Cape Cod, milk from the local dairy cooperative, and practically everything else from California. I have stood in line at fast food restaurants waiting to consume made-in-America hamburgers, french fries, and milk shakes. To me, America the beautiful was one big cafeteria.

When I became a chef, the cafeteria walls came tumbling down. I tasted and experimented with ingredients that thrived far beyond our shores, and I yearned to learn more. In other parts of the world, people picked mangoes off trees like we picked apples. They fried odd-looking bananas (plantains) like potatoes. Kiwis were eaten like strawberries and papayas like cantaloupes. The mild green pepper I grew up on was a snooze button compared to the 4-alarm chili peppers people in other parts of the world devoured.

I am not alone in my new-found appetite for the exotic. Food magazines have been trumpeting the recent influx of Thai, Polynesian, Mediterranean, Japanese, Caribbean, and Portuguese cooking. Many restaurant menus reflect this trend as they fuse disparate cuisines together and blur their descriptions. The increased availability of exotic foods at the marketplace further brings the international borders closer to home.

It is natural for our country to become a gastronomic melting pot. After all, we are more likely to recognize the cuisine of another country than its state flag or location on the map. Our country loves to eat, and we relate to other people through food.

All of this has induced today's cook to become less inhibited and to rely more on an international pantry. Jalapeño and serrano chili peppers, ginger root, daikon, cilantro, and lemongrass tumble out of refrigerators. Rice wine vinegar, mirin, coconut milk, tahini, and chili-garlic paste share shelf space with specialty vinegars, oil, and soy sauce.

This chapter offers a treasure of the diverse and eclectic condiments found across the world: the piquant pepper sauces of the Caribbean, the soothing raitas of India, the lime-soy-peanut pastes of Indonesia, the herbed tahini sauce from the Middle East, and the fiery harissa from North Africa are just some of the condiments included here.

Many of these condiments are easy to prepare, and the ingredients can be purchased at a supermarket or specialty foods store. Besides, not all international cuisines require exotic ingredients. Raita, a cooling Indian condiment, is a blend of cucumbers and yogurt. A spicy Indonesian paste is made with peanut butter. Creole sauce is, at first glance, prepared like a chunky tomato sauce.

All that these condiments require are a little less inhibition, a bit of daring, and a craving for something new and exciting.

Red Chili Sauce

Red chili sauces are prevalent in Thai, Indian, American Southwestern, Latin American, North African, and Chinese cuisines. They are usually extremely hot, coming at you full tilt from an inferno. This version introduces red bell peppers to temper the searing edge of red chilies, and the result is a slightly sweet and hot combination. Delicate, but with gusto.

Serve it with grilled or broiled fish or chicken, or as a colorful dip for vegetables.

4 to 6 dried red chili peppers
2 tablespoons butter
2 large red bell peppers, seeded and
    coarsely diced
1 medium-size onion, diced
3 to 4 garlic cloves, minced
3 to 4 fresh red chili or jalapeño
    peppers, seeded and minced
1¼ cups dry white wine
¼ cup water
1 tablespoon minced fresh cilantro
½ tablespoon dried thyme leaves
¼ teaspoon salt

Soak the dried chili peppers in warm water to cover for about 30 minutes. Once they are soft, remove their seeds and mince them.

Melt the butter in a saucepan. Add the red bell peppers, onion, garlic, and the fresh and dried chili peppers; sauté over medium heat, until the peppers are soft and the onions are opaque, about 10 minutes. Add the wine, water, cilantro, thyme, and salt. Bring the sauce to a simmer and cook over low heat for 15 to 20 minutes, or until the wine is reduced to half, stirring occasionally. In a food processor fitted with a steel blade or in a blender, puree the chili sauce until smooth.

Serve immediately or refrigerate. If kept refrigerated, the sauce should keep for 7 to 10 days.

YIELD: ABOUT 2½ CUPS

Creole Sauce

✦✦✦

It is fitting that Creole cooking originated in New Orleans, a city that celebrates life with extravagant parades at funerals, strolling jazz musicians, open-air trolley cars, Mardi Gras, and French Quarter saloons that stay open till dawn. While Cajun cooking is old French country cooking adapted to Louisiana's native ingredients, Creole cooking is a complex mixture of French, Spanish, Italian, American Indian, and African cuisines. It reflects the zest and spiciness of "the city that care forgot."

1 tablespoon butter
½ tablespoon vegetable oil
½ green pepper, seeded and diced
1 small onion, diced

1 small tomato, diced
¼ cup minced celery
¼ cup chopped okra
1 to 2 garlic cloves, minced
1 cup canned crushed tomatoes
¼ cup plus 2 tablespoons water
2 tablespoons dry red wine
1 tablespoon Worcestershire sauce
½ tablespoon dried oregano
1 teaspoon dried parsley
1 to 2 teaspoons red hot sauce
¼ teaspoon onion powder
¼ teaspoon salt
⅛ teaspoon black pepper
⅛ teaspoon white pepper
¼ teaspoon cayenne pepper
⅛ teaspoon red pepper flakes

✧✧✧

Heat the butter and oil in a saucepan. Add the green pepper, onion, fresh tomato, celery, okra, and garlic; sauté over moderately high heat for 10 to 12 minutes, reducing the heat to medium after about 5 minutes. The vegetables should be slightly cooked and still firm.

Reduce the heat to low and add the remaining ingredients to the pan. Bring the sauce to a simmer and continue to cook for 15 to 20 minutes, stirring frequently. Reduce the heat as the sauce thickens.

Serve the sauce immediately or refrigerate. If refrigerated, the sauce should keep for 7 to 10 days.

YIELD: 2 CUPS

Caribbean Pepper Sauce

❖❖

The British, Dutch, French, Chinese, Indian, Spanish, and African people have all contributed to the grand culinary mosaic known as Caribbean cuisine. Subtly sweet and fiery hot, many dishes rely on Scotch bonnet peppers (which are similar to habañero peppers), mangoes, papayas, plantains, homegrown spices, such as all-spice berries and nutmeg, and tamarind pulp, which yields a juice that is a cross between herbal tea and sour prunes. This pepper sauce is similar to a piquant, sweet and spicy barbecue sauce and should be smothered over grilled chicken or fish or steamed or grilled vegetables.

1 cup water
4 ounces dried tamarind pulp
4 to 6 Scotch bonnet, habañero, or
    jalapeño peppers, seeded and minced
2 tomatoes, diced
1 mango, peeled, pitted, and diced
1 medium-size onion, diced
2 to 3 garlic cloves, minced
¾ cup red wine vinegar
¼ cup brown sugar
14 to 16 allspice berries, crushed
½ teaspoon salt

Combine the water and tamarind and set aside for 3 to 4 hours, stirring occasionally. Drain through a sieve. Save the tamarind juice and discard the pulp.

✧✧

Combine the juice with the peppers, tomatoes, mango, onion, garlic, vinegar, sugar, and seasonings in a nonreactive saucepan. Cook over medium heat, stirring occasionally, for 25 to 30 minutes, or until the sauce is thick and chunky. Remove the sauce from the heat and set aside for 10 minutes. Puree in a food processor fitted with a steel blade or in a blender for 20 to 30 seconds, or until the sauce is smooth.

Serve the sauce immediately or refrigerate. If refrigerated, the sauce should keep for 1 to 2 weeks.

YIELD: 3 CUPS

Harissa

✦✦

Harissa is a fiery North African chili paste. It can be served in small quantities as a vegetable dip, passed at the table with strongly flavored fish, or blended with mayonnaise or sour cream and served with roasted chicken and cold meats. It also adds zip to rice and couscous. I like to spread it over a steak or grilled chicken sandwich, and wash it down with a cold beer.

3 to 4 fresh red chili or jalapeño
    peppers, seeded and minced
2 garlic cloves, minced
¼ cup canned crushed tomatoes
½ tablespoon ground cumin
½ tablespoon ground coriander
3 tablespoons olive oil

1 tablespoon lemon juice
2 to 3 teaspoons dried red pepper flakes

Combine all of the ingredients in a bowl and mix well. Serve immediately or wrap and chill. If refrigerated, the harissa should keep for 1 to 2 weeks.

YIELD: ½ CUP

Spicy Lime Peanut Sauce

Peanut butter combines with soy sauce, lime juice, ginger root, and hot peppers to form a very strong, complex taste. It has garnered kind of a cult following at my restaurant: customers spread it over bread, spoon it on a salad, even ask for a banana to spread it on. The sauce makes a jazzy accompaniment to mildly flavored fish or chicken dishes and satays.

½ cup crunchy unsalted peanut butter
¼ cup soy sauce
3 tablespoons lime juice
2 teaspoons sesame oil
½ teaspoon hot sesame oil
¼ cup unsalted peanuts
4 garlic cloves, minced
1 teaspoon minced fresh ginger root
¼ teaspoon red pepper flakes

Combine all of the ingredients in a food processor fitted with a steel blade and blend for 10 to 15 seconds, scraping the side of the bowl at least once. Or blend by hand by folding the peanut butter into the rest of the ingredients until fully incorporated.

Serve at room temperature. If refrigerated, the sauce should keep for about 2 weeks. Stir before serving.

YIELD: 1 CUP

Herbed Tahini Sauce

Tahini is a sesame paste with the consistency of natural peanut butter. It is best stored in a cool, dark place at room temperature. Tahini has a tendency to separate over time, but don't panic; simply stir it before using. Its nutty aftertaste and smooth texture blend well with yogurt, lemon, and fresh herbs. Almost any combination of fresh herbs will do, and I've listed a few of my favorites. Serve this sauce over broiled or grilled fish or chicken, steamed vegetables, or as a salad dressing.

1 cup tahini
1 cup plain yogurt
¼ cup lemon juice
1 to 2 garlic cloves, minced

1 tablespoon minced fresh mint
1 tablespoon minced fresh chives
1 tablespoon minced fresh marjoram
¼ teaspoon salt
⅛ teaspoon cayenne pepper

Combine all of the ingredients in a bowl and mix together. Serve immediately or wrap and chill. If refrigerated, the condiment should keep for 3 to 4 days.

YIELD: 2½ CUPS

Greek Yogurt Sauce

❖❖

With just a hint of dill and garlic, this cooling condiment is an adaptation of the Greek dish tzatsiki. I added the feta and spinach to create a stronger, more complex taste that balances spicy dishes while maintaining a distinctive presence of its own. Serve with roast lamb or pork, curry dishes, and shish kabobs. I like to spoon it over Vinaigrette-Grilled Chicken (page 109).

1 cup sour cream
1 cup plain yogurt
1 tablespoon red wine vinegar
3 garlic cloves, minced
1 medium-size unwaxed cucumber,
   diced (do not peel)
2 cups spinach leaves, washed and
   stemmed

1 tablespoon minced fresh dill weed
¼ teaspoon salt
¼ teaspoon black pepper
⅓ pound feta cheese

Combine all of the ingredients, except the feta, in a food processor fitted with a steel blade and process for 5 to 10 seconds. Pour into a serving bowl and mix the feta cheese into the sauce. Chill for 2 hours before serving. If refrigerated, the sauce should keep for 4 to 5 days.

YIELD: 3 CUPS

Mint Raita

✦✦✦

Raita is an Indian condiment that soothes the tongue, a cooling blend of plain yogurt and fruit or vegetables and spices. Raita is a nice accompaniment to most spicy dishes, and it is ideal for dousing the heat ignited by spicy chutneys and curry dishes. If possible, use cucumbers that have not been waxed.

1 cup plain yogurt
1 cup diced cucumbers (do not peel)
¼ cup sour cream
¼ cup chopped fresh mint leaves
½ teaspoon ground cumin
¼ teaspoon salt
⅛ teaspoon cayenne pepper

Combine all of the ingredients in a food processor fitted with a steel blade and process for 10 seconds. If you are blending by hand, finely chop the cucumbers and mint leaves and fold together with the remaining ingredients. Chill for at least 1 hour before serving. If refrigerated, the raita should keep for 4 to 5 days.

YIELD: 2 CUPS

Banana Raita

✦✦

This is a twist on the traditional Indian raita made with cucumbers. The bananas offer a nuance of sweetness, nicely balanced by the subtle bite of radishes and cilantro. Serve this raita with spicy dishes, such as Vegetables with Fiery Chutney (page 122), Chicken Indienne (page 115), Curried Chicken with Pineapple (page 114), and Blackened Eggplant (page 160).

1 cup plain yogurt
¼ cup sour cream
1 banana, peeled and diced
1 cup diced cucumber (do not peel)
2 to 3 radishes, washed and halved
1 tablespoon chopped fresh cilantro
½ teaspoon ground cumin
¼ teaspoon salt
⅛ teaspoon cayenne pepper

Combine all of the ingredients in a food processor fitted with a steel blade and process for 5 seconds. Scrape the sides of the bowl and process for another 5 seconds. If you are blending by hand, mash the bananas and cucumber together; mince the radish, and fold in with the remaining ingredients.

Pour the raita into a serving dish and chill for at least 1 hour before serving. If refrigerated, the raita should keep for 4 to 5 days.

YIELD: 2½ CUPS

Black Bean Soup with Mint Raita

A good black bean soup has a nourishing, stick-to-your-ribs quality, and it is the sort of sustenance that I crave most in wintertime. Black beans have an earthy taste that blends well with cumin, garlic, chili peppers, and cilantro. The Mint Raita offers a cooling contrast to these distinctive southwestern flavors.

8 ounces black beans, washed and
   soaked overnight
7 to 8 cups vegetable stock or water
2 tablespoons red wine
½ cup flat beer
2 medium-size onions, diced
4 garlic cloves, minced
2 tablespoons butter

1 cup finely chopped celery
1 green pepper, seeded and diced
1 red bell pepper, seeded and diced
2 jalapeño peppers, seeded and minced
2 large carrots, peeled and diced
½ cup canned crushed tomatoes
1½ tablespoons ground cumin
1 teaspoon red hot sauce
½ tablespoon chili powder
½ teaspoon black pepper
½ teaspoon salt
¼ teaspoon cayenne pepper
1 tablespoon minced fresh cilantro
2 cups Mint Raita (page 142)

Drain the black beans and combine with the stock, wine, beer, 1 of the onions, and garlic and bring to a simmer. Cook for 1 to 2 hours over low heat, stirring occasionally. If the stock evaporates too quickly, reduce the heat, add up to 2 cups of hot water, and continue simmering.

Melt the butter in a saucepan and add the remaining onion, celery, peppers, and carrots. Sauté over medium heat until the vegetables are soft but not mushy, 5 to 7 minutes. Set aside.

When the beans are soft, puree half of the mixture in a food processor fitted with a steel blade. Return the beans to the pan, add the sautéed vegetables, crushed tomatoes, seasonings, and cilantro to the pan. Bring to a simmer and cook for about 15 minutes, stirring occasionally. Add a little hot water if it is too thick, or continue to simmer if it is too thin.

Serve at once in soup bowls and spoon Mint Raita over the top.

YIELD: 4 TO 8 SERVINGS

Tandoori-Grilled Tuna

❖❖❖

Tandoori cooking, an Indian tradition, refers to food marinated in yogurt and herbs and then baked in a tandoori oven or pit. The yogurt marinade tenderizes the meat and imparts subtle flavors of cumin, ginger, and garlic. This recipe adapts the tandoori style of cooking to the American barbecue. The light flavor of grilled tuna is enhanced by the marinade, and the chutney and raita complement it as well.

10 to 12 garlic cloves, minced
1 jalapeño pepper, seeded and minced
2 tablespoons ground cumin
2 tablespoons ground coriander
1 tablespoon paprika
1 teaspoon ground cloves
1 teaspoon black pepper
1 teaspoon salt
1 teaspoon red hot sauce
½ teaspoon cayenne pepper

Tandoori Marinade

2 cups plain yogurt
½ cup olive oil
¼ cup red wine vinegar
2 tablespoons minced fresh ginger root

Fish

1½ pounds tuna steaks, cut ½ inch thick
1½ cups raita (pages 142 and 143)
1½ cups Mango Chutney (page 76), or
   Rhubarb Chutney (page 83)

146

✤✤✤

In a mixing bowl, combine all of the ingredients for the marinade and whisk well. Place the tuna steaks in a shallow dish and cover with the tandoori marinade. Refrigerate for 4 hours, turning the fish once.

Preheat the grill until the coals are gray to white. Raise the grill at least 6 inches from the heat.

Remove the tuna from the marinade and pat dry. Lightly oil the grill and place tuna steaks over the heat; turn after 5 to 7 minutes. Continue grilling for another 5 minutes or until the tuna is pale brown or burgundy in the center.

Ladle ½ cup of raita onto each of 4 warm dinner plates and set the tuna in the center. Serve immediately and pass the chutney or relish at the table.

Note: The food colors that give tandoori dishes a bright pink color have been omitted. If you want the color, a few drops of red and yellow food coloring will do the trick.

YIELD: 4 SERVINGS

Lobster-Spinach Crêpes

❖❖❖

Although crêpes are thought of as a light meal, too often the filling is bound with a roux (a mixture of butter and flour), which leaves one feeling quite full. Red chili sauce blends well with lobster, scallops, and shrimp and requires only a little cheese and light cream to bind the ingredients together.

Spinach Crêpes

3 eggs, beaten
1½ cups unbleached all-purpose flour
1½ cups milk
¼ teaspoon salt
⅛ teaspoon cayenne pepper
6 tablespoons melted butter
¾ cup chopped fresh spinach leaves
2 tablespoons butter

Filling

1 tablespoon butter
1 green pepper, seeded and diced
2 (1-pound) lobsters, cooked and meat removed
½ cup Red Chili Sauce (page 132)
2 tablespoons light cream
½ cup corn kernels, fresh, canned, or frozen and thawed
1 cup shredded provolone or Monterey jack cheese

To make the crêpes, combine the eggs, flour, milk, salt, and cayenne pepper in a large mixing bowl. Fold in the 6 tablespoons of melted butter and the spinach leaves and refrigerate for 1 hour.

Melt 1 tablespoon of the remaining butter in an 8-inch crêpe pan or skillet and ladle about ½ cup of batter into the pan. Tilt the pan to ease the batter around the base of the pan and form a thin, round pancake. When the edges of the crêpe are light brown, flip the crêpe with a smooth motion. Continue cooking until the surface is light brown and then remove to a warm plate.

Cook the remaining batter in the same fashion, adding about a teaspoon of butter to the pan after cooking each crêpe. Cover the finished crêpes with waxed paper.

To make the filling, melt the butter over moderately high heat in a large skillet. Add the green pepper and sauté for 2 to 3 minutes. Then stir in the lobster meat. Continue cooking until the green pepper is soft but not mushy. Add the Red Chili Sauce, cream, and corn and bring the mixture to a simmer. Simmer for about 30 seconds, stir in the cheese, and continue to cook until the cheese fully melts. Remove the mixture from the heat.

Place a crêpe on each of 4 dinner plates. Spoon a quarter of the filling on each, forming a log in the middle of each crêpe. Wrap the crêpe around the filling and serve immediately with steamed vegetables.

YIELD: 4 SERVINGS

Chicken Satays

A satay is a marinated and grilled dish that is served with a spicy condiment. In many Indonesian dishes, soy sauce, lime juice, peanut butter, coconut milk, spicy seasonings, and chili pastes are frequently used in either the marinade or the condiment. I prefer a coconut milk marinade spiced with cilantro, chili-garlic paste, and lemongrass (a crunchy, citrusy herb prevalent in Thai cuisine). The marinade tenderizes the meat and yields a mild coconut nuance with a dash of spiciness. Serve it with Spicy Lime Peanut Sauce or with a sweet-and-sour condiment, such as Caribbean Pepper Sauce or Rhubarb-Plum Catsup. Beef, pork, shrimp, and scallops also make excellent satays.

2 cups unsweetened coconut milk
  (see note opposite)
¼ cup rice wine vinegar
1 fresh lemongrass stalk, diced,
  or 1 tablespoon grated lime zest
2 tablespoons chili-garlic paste
  (available where Oriental foods
  are sold)
1½ tablespoons minced fresh cilantro
1 pound boneless and skinless chicken
  breasts, pounded and cut into 2-inch-
  wide strips
½ cup Spicy Lime Peanut Sauce
  (page 139)
½ cup Caribbean Pepper Sauce
  (page 136) or Rhubarb-Plum Catsup
  (page 72) (optional)

Combine the coconut milk, vinegar, lemongrass, chili paste, and cilantro in a bowl.

Thread the chicken strips onto 10-inch metal or bamboo skewers and place in a casserole dish. Pour the marinade over the skewers and chill for 2 hours. Turn the skewers after marinating for 1 hour.

Preheat the grill until the coals are gray to white.

When the coals are ready, place the skewers on the grill. Turn the skewers occasionally and cook for 7 to 10 minutes, or until the chicken is white in the center.

Remove the skewers to warm plates and serve immediately with Spicy Lime Peanut Sauce and Caribbean Pepper Sauce or Rhubarb-Plum Catsup. Herbed Couscous (page 168) makes a nice accompaniment if the satays are served as a dinner.

Note: You can buy coconut milk where Oriental foods are sold or you can make your own. Poke a hole in one end of a coconut and drain the liquid into a cup. Strain the liquid and set it aside. Crack and peel the coconut and shred the meat in a blender until it becomes liquidy. Add the reserved coconut water along with 2 to 4 cups of boiling hot water (depending on how strong you want it) to the blended coconut meat, cover and let stand for 30 minutes, and then strain out.

A half of a coconut will yield 2 to 4 cups of coconut milk, depending on how rich a milk you want.

YIELD: 4 APPETIZER OR 2 DINNER SERVINGS

Chicken Wings with 3 Sauces

✦✦

Who'd have thought chicken wings would put Buffalo, New York, on the culinary map? Buffalo is where chicken wings were elevated from a little-used chicken by-product to a chic finger food that would be offered on menus across the country, from neighborhood taverns to fashionable dinner houses. The original Buffalo-style wings were fried, doused with an extremely hot concoction, and served with celery sticks and blue cheese dressing. Another popular way to prepare wings is to marinate the chicken wings in soy and ginger and bake or broil them. Serve the wings with a variety of condiments.

2 cups soy sauce
1½ cups vegetable oil
1 cup Worcestershire sauce
1 cup orange juice
2 tablespoons honey
2 tablespoons minced fresh ginger root
6 to 8 garlic cloves, minced
3 teaspoons hot sesame oil or red hot sauce
2 teaspoons dried red pepper flakes
2 teaspoons black pepper
24 to 30 chicken wings, tips removed (about 4½ pounds)
1 head leaf lettuce, cored and washed
1 cup Apricot-Peach Catsup (page 74) or Cherry Tomato-Date Catsup (page 73)
1 cup Creole Sauce (page 134)
1 cup Greek Yogurt Sauce (page 141) or Mint Raita (page 142)

Whisk together the soy sauce, oil, Worcestershire sauce, orange juice, honey, ginger, garlic, hot oil, dried red pepper flakes, and black pepper. Add the chicken wings and refrigerate for 3 to 6 hours, stirring the marinade after about 2 hours.

Preheat the oven to 375° F. Remove the wings from the marinade and place them on a rack over a pan. Bake until they are browned, about 15 to 20 minutes.

Arrange the finished chicken wings on leaf lettuce and serve immediately with the 3 sauces.

YIELD: 4 TO 6 APPETIZER SERVINGS

Myers Heights Shish Kabobs

I grew up near Cayuga Lake, one of New York's Finger Lakes, and during the summer my family would often grill shish kabobs near the lake's shore. My father or uncle would use my grandmother's large, homemade pita bread to turn the kabobs on the grill, and when the kabobs were done cooking, they'd use the bread to slide them off the skewers. After 6 or 7 skewers, the bread would be soaked with delicious meat and onion juices. We'd tear up the bread into small pieces, pinch the kabobs, and dip the whole thing into a garlic and oil mixture. The Greek Yogurt Sauce is a natural accompaniment to lamb, and I couldn't resist including this family tradition in my cookbook.

6 to 8 garlic cloves, minced
½ cup olive oil
2 pounds leg of lamb, trimmed and cut
    into 1-inch cubes
1 large onion, coarsely chopped
1 large green pepper, seeded and
    coarsely chopped
2 tomatoes, cut into 8 wedges
4 warmed pita breads, halved
½ head leaf lettuce, torn
1½ cups Greek Yogurt Sauce (page 141)

Preheat the grill until the coals are gray to white.

Combine the garlic and the oil in a shallow mixing bowl and set aside.

Skewer the lamb cubes, onion, green

pepper, and tomatoes, alternating the lamb between each vegetable. When the grill is ready, place the skewers on the grill. Turn the skewers occasionally and cook until the lamb is brown to light burgundy in the center, 7 to 10 minutes.

Remove the skewers from the heat and slide the lamb and vegetables off the skewers and into the garlic-oil marinade. Coat the grilled ingredients thoroughly and let stand for 3 to 5 minutes.

Stuff the pita breads with the leaf lettuce, fork the lamb and vegetables into the stuffed pita, and spoon the Greek Yogurt Sauce over it. Serve immediately.

YIELD: 4 SERVINGS

Ragin' Cajun Burger

+++

Years ago I was a dishwasher at a bar and grill. When the grill cook failed to show up on New Year's Eve, I was handed the spatula. Granted, I had won a Silver Spatula award from McDonald's a few years back, but grilling 15 to 20 hamburgers and steaks at once, each cooked to the customer's wishes, was a whole new ballgame. I was exasperated and felt that I would never master the craft of grilling. Nonetheless, I was given the job and eventually learned the difference between medium-rare and medium-well. This Ragin' Cajun Burger reminds me of those early days filled with hamburgers, steaks, and fries.

1½ pounds ground beef
1 green pepper, seeded and minced
1 medium-size onion, minced
2 jalapeño peppers, seeded and minced
1 tablespoon red hot sauce
2 teaspoons dried oregano
1 teaspoon red pepper flakes
½ to 1 teaspoon cayenne pepper or
   Blackened Seasonings (page 167)
4 (1-ounce) slices provolone cheese
4 warmed hamburger rolls
6 tablespoons Creole Sauce (page 134)
1 large tomato, sliced
4 to 5 leaves leaf or romaine lettuce,
   torn

✛✛

Combine the beef, green pepper, onion, and jalapeño peppers in a large bowl. Mix in the red hot sauce and seasonings and shape the meat into 4 burger patties.

Grill or panfry the burgers until cooked to the desired doneness. Melt 1 slice of cheese on each burger a few seconds before placing them on the warmed buns. Spoon about 1½ tablespoons of Creole Sauce onto each burger and top each with tomato and lettuce. Serve with Roasted Garlic Potatoes (page 128) or a tossed salad.

YIELD: 4 SERVINGS

Veggie Jambalaya with Mint Raita

In college, I lived in a housing cooperative called Watermargin, and with all of my housemates, I managed and maintained the house and staffed our own kitchen. As kitchen steward, I helped plan meals for 25 people and soon found that with limited resources, it was not an easy job accommodating 10 vegetarians and 15 carnivores. In the past, meat-eaters had occasionally gorged on prime rib while the vegetarians were offered barley soup and bread. The vegetarians lobbied for meals that would be just as hearty as the meat dishes, and they inspired dishes like the Veggie Jambalaya, a meal that retains the spirit and heartiness of the traditional meat dish but substitutes a cornucopia of vegetables in lieu of meat.

4 tablespoons butter
12 broccoli florets, blanched
2 green peppers, seeded and diced
1 medium-size carrot, peeled and
   shredded
16 mushrooms, sliced
1 small zucchini, diced
1 cup corn kernels, fresh, canned, or
   frozen and thawed
5½ cups Creole Sauce (page 134)
6 cups cooked white rice
2 cups Mint Raita (page 142)

Melt the butter in a large sauté pan over moderate heat and add all of the vegetables, except the corn. Sauté for 7 to 10 minutes, or until the vegetables are soft but not mushy.

✿✿✿

Add the corn and Creole Sauce to the pan and bring the mixture to a simmer. Continue to simmer for 1 minute, stirring frequently.

Place 1½ cups of rice in the center of each plate and pour the Creole mixture over the rice. Spoon about ¼ cup of Mint Raita over each jambalaya and serve at once.

YIELD: 4 TO 6 SERVINGS

Blackened Eggplant with Raita

The flavor and texture of eggplant blends well with a variety of seasonings and sauces and is great for grilling. The first bite of Blackened Eggplant gives the thrilling sensation of the fiery seasonings; then the second bite is cooled and tempered by the raita. Serve the eggplant as a side dish or over fresh greens as a warm dinner salad with Dijon-Style Mustard Vinaigrette (page 165) and mixed vegetables.

1 medium-size eggplant, cut into ¼-inch
   horizontal slices (do not peel)
½ cup olive oil
1 to 2 tablespoons Blackened
   Seasonings (page 167)
2 tablespoons butter (if eggplant is
   panfried)

2 cups Banana Raita (page 143) or Mint
   Raita (page 142)

Preheat the grill until the coals are gray to white.

In a shallow dish, brush both sides of the eggplant slices with the oil. When the coals are ready, place the slices on the grill.

Shake the seasonings over the eggplant slices as they cook. Turn the them after about 3 minutes, and season the other sides. Continue grilling for another 3 minutes, or until the eggplant slices are softening and browning slightly. (Add more seasonings if you prefer a hotter sensation.)

If you are panfrying the eggplant, melt 2 tablespoons of butter in a large skillet. Add

✛✛

the eggplant slices to the pan and sprinkle the seasonings over the slices as they cook. Turn after 5 to 7 minutes, or when the slices are slightly brown. Shake more seasonings over the eggplant and cook for another 3 to 5 minutes.

Serve the eggplant slices immediately. Spoon the raita over the top and pass the extra raita at the table.

YIELD: 3 TO 4 SERVINGS

Herbed Artichokes

❖❖❖

For those who cherish the artichoke, peeling its outer leaves is a labor of love. I like to dip the leaves in a garlicky condiment, such as Herbed Tahini Sauce or Basil Aioli. At the center of the artichoke, hidden beneath a mass of purple leaves and choke (a brush-like covering), lies the reward for one's efforts, the sumptuous heart. Serve the artichokes as a prelude to an elegant meal, or as a treat with soup, salad, and Pumpkin Scones with Chutney (page 126).

4 whole artichokes, stems removed
4 lemon slices
1 teaspoon salt
1½ cups Herbed Tahini Sauce (page 140) or Basil Aioli (page 40)
1 lemon, quartered

Snugly fit the artichokes, stem side down, inside a stainless steel or porcelain-lined saucepan. Add the lemon slices and salt. Pour in boiling water to cover. Boil for 35 to 45 minutes or until the artichoke bottoms are easily pierced with a fork. Remove the artichokes with tongs and place them upside down in a colander to drain.

To serve, place each artichoke in a small bowl. Pass the Herbed Tahini Sauce or Basil Aioli at the table.

YIELD: 4 SERVINGS

5
Extras

❖❖

Cashew Pesto

❖❖

Pesto was first made by natives of Genoa, Italy. The highly flavored herb paste was crushed together with mortar and pestle (hence the name pesto). I prefer pesto made with cashews, but pine nuts or walnuts can be substituted. Dried basil, however, cannot be substituted for fresh basil; the difference between fresh basil and dried basil is the difference between lightning and a lightning bug.

12 to 16 garlic cloves
1½ cups unsalted raw cashews
3 cups fresh basil leaves
3 cups fresh spinach leaves
¾ cup olive or other vegetable oil
2 cups freshly grated Parmesan cheese

¼ teaspoon salt
¼ teaspoon black pepper

In a food processor, combine the garlic, cashews, basil, spinach, and oil. Process until a paste is formed. Remove the paste to a bowl and fold in the cheese and seasonings.

Use the pesto immediately or cover with a thin layer of olive oil to exclude air. Wrap and chill. If refrigerated, the pesto should keep for about 2 weeks.

YIELD: 3 CUPS

Dijon-Style Mustard Vinaigrette

✦✦✦

Vinaigrette is the marriage of oil and vinegar. It is easy to prepare and makes an ideal dressing for fresh vegetable salads. Substituting specialty vinegars, such as balsamic, raspberry, or sherry, in lieu of the red wine vinegar, adds a delightful nuance to the dressing.

½ cup olive or other vegetable oil
¼ cup red wine vinegar
1 tablespoon Dijon-style mustard or
   Basic Mustard (page 41)
½ teaspoon black pepper
½ teaspoon sugar
½ teaspoon salt
½ teaspoon dried thyme
½ teaspoon dried tarragon

½ teaspoon dried oregano
½ teaspoon dried basil

Combine all the ingredients in a jar with a tight-fitting lid and shake for 10 seconds. Use immediately or refrigerate. Shake well before serving. If refrigerated, the vinaigrette should keep for 2 to 3 weeks.

YIELD: ¾ CUP

Papaya Guacamole

❖❖

This is a citrusy twist on traditional guacamole. A special feature of this preparation is that the guacamole doesn't brown as fast as usual, since the high citrus content of the papaya slows down the oxidation (browning) process. The avocados should be ripe and give slightly when pressed. Serve guacamole with stuffed tortillas, tacos, grilled chicken and fish, and as a topping for salad.

2 avocados, peeled and diced
1 papaya, peeled, halved, seeded, and
   diced
1 large tomato, diced
1 red onion, diced
2 to 3 garlic cloves, minced
2 to 3 jalapeño peppers, seeded and
   minced

1 tablespoon minced fresh cilantro
¼ cup lime juice
1 tablespoon ground cumin
1 teaspoon red hot sauce
¼ teaspoon salt
¼ teaspoon black pepper
¼ teaspoon white pepper

Combine all of the ingredients in a food processor and process for 5 to 10 seconds. Scrape the sides; process for another 10 seconds, or until the guacamole forms a chunky paste. Serve at once or refrigerate. If kept refrigerated, the guacamole should keep for 3 to 4 days.

YIELD: 3 CUPS

Blackened Seasonings

"Blackening" a fish has proven to be more than a passing fad. The seasonings have become as routine as salt and pepper. Like curry powder and chili powder, blackened seasonings are a mixture of hot and mild spices. For more heat, add cayenne pepper; for a milder mixture, add chili powder, thyme, or onion powder. Sprinkle blackened seasonings over any type of grilled or panfried fish, chicken, beef, or vegetable.

2 tablespoons chili powder
1 tablespoon cayenne pepper
1 tablespoon black pepper
1 tablespoon white pepper
½ tablespoon ground cumin
½ tablespoon paprika
½ tablespoon onion powder
½ tablespoon ground thyme

Combine all of the seasonings in a small mixing bowl. Spoon into a container with a sieve-top lid. Store in a cool, dry place.

YIELD: ABOUT ½ CUP

Herbed Couscous

❖❖

Couscous is a rice-like pasta that is quick and easy to prepare. It makes a light side dish to accompany chicken, turkey, fish, and vegetable entrées.

1 cup uncooked couscous
½ cup minced onion
¼ cup raisins
¼ cup slivered blanched almonds
1 teaspoon dried oregano
1 teaspoon dried basil
1 teaspoon dried tarragon
1 teaspoon dried chives
½ teaspoon dried rosemary
½ teaspoon salt
½ teaspoon black pepper
2 tablespoons butter
1½ cups boiling water

Combine the couscous, onion, raisins, almonds, and seasonings in a mixing bowl and set aside.

Add the butter to the boiling water. Pour over the couscous and stir thoroughly. Cover and set aside for 5 minutes.

Fluff the couscous with a fork and serve immediately.

YIELD: 4 TO 5 SIDE DISH SERVINGS

Basic Black Beans

✧✧✧

*Black beans add earthy flavor and suste-
nance to stuffed tortillas, salsas, jam-
balayas, soups, and stir-fries. Uncooked
black beans should be sorted for rocks and
washed prior to cooking. Soaking the beans
overnight will decrease the cooking time,
but I always forget to soak them, so this
recipe is for unsoaked black beans.
Although many recipes call for chicken
stock or ham hocks added to the beans, I
prefer vegetable stock or water. I also like
to add a sprig of cilantro or a minced jalapeño pepper, but that's up to you.*

1 cup uncooked washed, and sorted
   black beans
3½ cups warm water or vegetable stock
½ cup dry red wine
½ cup diced onion

2 to 3 garlic cloves, minced
1 tablespoon ground cumin
2 teaspoons chili powder
½ teaspoon red hot sauce
½ teaspoon salt
¼ teaspoon black pepper
⅛ teaspoon cayenne pepper

Combine all of the ingredients in a saucepan
and cook over low heat, stirring occasionally, for 40 to 45 minutes, or until the beans
are soft. Remove from the heat and set aside
for 10 minutes.

Serve warm or refrigerate until you are
ready to use them. If refrigerated, the black
beans should keep for 5 to 7 days.

YIELD: ABOUT 3 CUPS

169

6
Notes on Canning

Thrift and preservation have long been American ideals. The craft of canning grew out of the urge to preserve and conserve. Canning prolongs the life of certain fruits, vegetables, jams, relishes, and chutneys by destroying the enzymes and microorganisms that cause spoilage.

There are two common methods of canning: boiling water bath and steam pressure canning. Boiling water bath canning raises the temperature of the condiment to 212° F., adequate for ensuring the safety of high-acid ingredients—fruit, tomatoes, and vinegar-based condiments. Steam pressure canning is required for meat, chicken, seafood, and most vegetables. This book is only concerned with high-acid foods and the boiling water bath method.

The boiling water bath method is based on the following premises: Condiments are placed in sterilized jars, sealed airtight, immersed in boiling water for 10 to 20 minutes, and then cooled to room temperature. The combination of high-acid ingredients, vacuum sealing, and the exposure to high temperatures creates a safe, spoilage-free environment.

To use the boiling water bath method, you'll need the following equipment:

- Canning jars with screw bands and lids
- Large kettle and lid, equipped with a rack to keep the jars off the bottom of the pan and to keep them from bumping into each other.
- Canning funnel
- Rubber spatula
- Paper towels or clean kitchen towels
- Jar lifter (optional, but very handy)
- Timer
- High-acid condiment

Use only jars made specifically for canning. Commercial jars made for peanut butter or mayonnaise should not be used. They are not heat tempered, often have nicks in them, and do not always form an airtight seal.

Once you have all of the equipment handy, make the condiment. When the condiment is cooking, start the canning process. Fill the kettle with water to a level that will cover the jars by at least 1 inch. Place the kettle over the heat and bring the water to a boil.

While the water is heating, examine the jars and lids for nicks or blemishes. Wash the jars, lids, and screw bands in hot, soapy water. Next, sanitize the jars and screw bands in a dishwasher or immerse them in boiling water for 10 minutes. Keep the jars in the hot water until you are ready to fill them. Follow the directions on the package for sanitizing the lids; do not boil.

When the condiment is ready, remove it from the heat. Use the jar lifter to remove the jars and lids from the water. Wipe and dry each jar, lid, and screw band with a clean towel and set on a clean towel. Fill each jar, one at a time, by placing the funnel over the jars and spooning in the condiment, leaving 1 inch of air space at the top. The air space allows the condiment to expand as it cooks in the water bath. Remove any air bubbles by sliding the rubber spatula around the inside wall of the jar.

Wipe the jar of any spilled condiment with a clean towel. Once the jar is filled, place the lid over the jar and fasten the screw band into place, turning it tight. Set the jar aside and repeat the process with the remaining condiment and jars.

When the water in the water bath is boiling, grip the jars with the jar lifter and place them in the water. Arrange them in the kettle so they are completely immersed and do not touch each other. Place a lid over the kettle. Set the timer from the time the water returns to a boil.

When the required time has elapsed, remove the jars from the water and set them upright.

Allow the jars to cool to room temperature before inspecting them for a proper seal.

For a proper seal, the jar lid should be slightly concave, indicating a good vacuum seal. You may hear a pinging sound as the condiment cools and the lid pops down. If the lid pops back up, there is no seal, so refrigerate the condiment and use within the recommended shelf life.

Label the jars with the date and condiment name. Store the sealed jars in a cool, dry, dark place.

For a more detailed description of canning, I recommend *Putting Food By* by Janet Greene, Ruth Hertzberg, and Beatrice Vaughan. I also found *Ball's Blue Book on Canning and Freezing* to be a valuable guide.

Index

7930   4491